CRIES OF THE SPIRIT

Best wishes at the
beginning of 1992 —
Jane Gentry

For Cyndi —
May this volume
lend you good company
On your personal journey
And the a resource journey
in your work —
Marta Sewell

Best wishes
listening
for light —

Marge Ella Lynn
1.5.92

CRIES OF THE SPIRIT

A CELEBRATION OF WOMEN'S SPIRITUALITY

Edited by Marilyn Sewell

Beacon Press   Boston

Beacon Press
25 Beacon Street
Boston, Massachusetts 02108-2800

Beacon Press books
are published under the auspices of
the Unitarian Universalist Association of Congregations.

This project was funded in part by
the Unitarian Universalist Denominational Grants Panel.

98 97 96 95 94 93 92 91   8 7 6 5 4

Text design by Lisa Diercks

Library of Congress Cataloging-in-Publication Data

Cries of the spirit: a celebration of women's spirituality/edited
by Marilyn Sewell.
p.   cm.
ISBN 0-8070-6812-8   ISBN 0-8070-6813-6 (pbk)
1. Christian literature, American—Women authors.   2. Women—
Religious life—Literary collections.   3. Christian literature—
Women authors.   I. Sewell, Marilyn.
PS509.C55C7   1991   90-52581
810.8'0382—dc20   CIP

For my sons, Kash and Madison

Contents

Preface / xv
Acknowledgments / xix
Introduction / 1

Owning Self

Unlearning to not Speak / Marge Piercy / 21
The woman in the ordinary / Marge Piercy / 21
Shameless Hussy (excerpt) / Alta / 22
Woman and Nature (excerpt) / Susan Griffin / 23
Variation on a Theme by Rilke / Denise Levertov / 23
Stepping Westward / Denise Levertov / 24
The Poem as Mask / Muriel Rukeyser / 25
Outrage / Lucille Iverson / 25
Woman in the Nineteenth Century (excerpt) / Margaret Fuller / 27
Offspring / Naomi Long Madgett / 28
Now I Become Myself / May Sarton / 28
i am running into a new year / Lucille Clifton / 29
Listen / Linda Lancione Moyer / 30
Lilith and the Doctor / Kathleen Norris / 30
The Journey / Mary Oliver / 31
The Irises / Jeanne Foster / 32
Blue Morning Glory / Anne Pitkin / 33
Housing Shortage / Naomi Replansky / 34
Aging (balm for a 27th birthday) / Erica Jong / 35
Advice / Ruth Stone / 37

The Imperative of Intimacy

Prayer for Revolutionary Love / Denise Levertov / 41
Out of My Time (excerpt) / Marya Mannes / 41
Councils / Marge Piercy / 42
To have without holding / Marge Piercy / 43
Paris and Helen / Judy Grahn / 44
Pornography and Silence (excerpt) / Susan Griffin / 45
Growing Together / Joyce Carol Oates / 45
After Love / Maxine Kumin / 46

A Thought / Linda Hogan / 47

New Mother / Sharon Olds / 48

*Dancing the Shout to the True Gospel or The Song Movement Sisters Don't Want
     Me to Sing* / Rita Mae Brown / 48

Late Autumn / May Sarton / 49

The Way Towards Each Other / Jeni Couzyn / 49

Blossom / Mary Oliver / 50

To Drink / Jane Hirshfield / 51

Medicine / Alice Walker / 51

Love Is Not Concerned / Alice Walker / 52

The Hug / Tess Gallagher / 52

Nikki-Rosa / Nikki Giovanni / 54

Feast Day (excerpt) / Ellen Bryant Voigt / 55

Ironing Their Clothes / Julia Alvarez / 55

7 : 3 (excerpt) / Alta / 56

2 : 7 (excerpt) / Alta / 56

The Big Heart / Anne Sexton / 57

Centering (excerpt) / Mary Caroline Richards / 58

Mothering

Advent / Kathleen Norris / 63

Early Morning Woman / Joy Harjo / 64

Poems for the New / Kathleen Fraser / 64

Magnificat / Chana Bloch / 65

The Wife Takes a Child / Ellen Bryant Voigt / 66

Birth / George Ella Lyon / 67

Rising to Meet It / Chana Bloch / 67

Now That I Am Forever with Child / Audre Lorde / 68

The Network of the Imaginary Mother (excerpt) / Robin Morgan / 69

The Network of the Imaginary Mother (excerpt) / Robin Morgan / 70

Lorelei / Alta / 71

Unspoken / Judith Ortiz Cofer / 71

Happy Birthday / Alicia Ostriker / 72

Mothers, Daughters / Shirley Kaufman / 73

The Bad Mother / Susan Griffin / 74

Black Mother Woman / Audre Lorde / 75

February 13, 1980 / Lucille Clifton / 75

One Writer's Beginnings (excerpt) / Eudora Welty / 76

The Measure of My Days (excerpt) / Florida Scott-Maxwell / 76

Mother / Sharon Mayer Libera / 77

Each Bird Walking / Tess Gallagher / 77

35/10 / Sharon Olds / 79

Dandelion Greens / Jane Flanders / *83*

Keeping Hair / Ramona Wilson / *83*

Matmiya / Mary TallMountain / *84*

For Two Who Slipped Away Almost Entirely / Alice Walker / *85*

Legacies / Nikki Giovanni / *86*

Whitecaps / Betsy Sholl / *87*

Lineage / Margaret Walker / *87*

Poem to My Grandmother in Her Death / Michele Murray / *88*

Five Poems for Grandmothers (excerpt) / Margaret Atwood / *89*

Spring Fragments (excerpt) / Betsy Sholl / *91*

Prologue (excerpt) / Audre Lorde / *91*

Poem at Thirty-nine / Alice Walker / *92*

The Envelope / Maxine Kumin / *93*

Eggs / Sharon Olds / *94*

The Moment / Sharon Olds / *95*

Three Sweatshop Women / Nanying Stella Wong / *95*

A Poem about Faith / Kathleen Norris / *96*

the will's love / Besmilr Brigham / *98*

What Is Repeated, What Abides / Barbara Hendryson / *98*

Elegy / Maya Angelou / *99*

Death and Lesser Losses

The Mother / Gwendolyn Brooks / *103*

ten years ago / Eileen Moeller / *104*

Unborn Child Elegy (excerpt) / Margaret Gibson / *105*

Country Woman Elegy / Margaret Gibson / *105*

Flowers / Kathleen Fraser / *106*

104. / Alta / *107*

3 : 1 / Alta / *108*

My Grandfather / Joanne Hotchkiss / *108*

Lynn / Jeanne Foster / *109*

Easter, 1968 / May Sarton / *110*

What Hell Is / Heather McHugh / *111*

Mama Rosanna's Last Bead-Clack / Laurel Speer / *113*

Lament / Edna St. Vincent Millay / *113*

"Goodnight, Willie Lee, I'll See You in the Morning" / Alice Walker / *114*

Finding the Lamb (excerpt) / Rebecca Newth / *114*

Aunt Lucy / Jane Gentry / *115*

Apples / Shirley Kaufman / *116*

In the House of the Dying / Jane Cooper / *117*

In Flight / Jennifer Regan / *118*

Grandmother / Marilyn Krysl / *118*

x   *Betrothed* / Louise Bogan / *120*

Some Slippery Afternoon / Daniela Gioseffi / *120*

Gift from the Sea (excerpt) / Anne Morrow Lindbergh / *121*

Waiting / Jane Cooper / *122*

The Cancer Journals (excerpt) / Audre Lorde / *123*

Gestalt at Sixty (excerpt) / May Sarton / *123*

Ebba Dawson: Mardel Rest Home, Haskell, New Jersey / Maria Gillan / *124*

The Measure of My Days (excerpt) / Florida Scott-Maxwell / *125*

Testimony / Jane Flanders / *126*

Planting Onions / Jane Flanders / *126*

Survivors / Chana Bloch / *127*

The Poem as a Reservoir for Grief (excerpt) / Tess Gallagher / *127*

In the Midst of Winter (excerpt) / Mary Jane Moffat / *128*

In Blackwater Woods / Mary Oliver / *128*

Anxiety about Dying / Alicia Ostriker / *129*

Sonnet 2 from "The Autumn Sonnets" / May Sarton / *130*

All Souls / May Sarton / *131*

Songs of Brokenness and Alienation

Crazy Quilt / Jane Wilson Joyce / *135*

Silence. She Is Six Years Old / Lynn Emanuel / *135*

Greg's Got Custody of Sally / Julia Alvarez / *136*

Meditations with Hildegard of Bingen (excerpt) / Hildegard of Bingen / *136*

The Journey (excerpt) / Lillian Smith / *137*

Solstice Poem (excerpt) / Margaret Atwood / *138*

Moving / Jeanne Foster / *138*

Misguided / Harriet Brown / *140*

Christmas Letter, 1970 (excerpt) / May Sarton / *140*

Town I Left / Helen Sorrells / *141*

S M / Alice Walker / *141*

My Mother, Who Came from China, Where She Never Saw Snow / Laureen Mar / *142*

Lady on a Bus / Jeanne Lohmann / *143*

I Check My Parents' House / Julia Alvarez / *144*

The History of My Feeling / Kathleen Fraser / *144*

Hand games / Marge Piercy / *146*

The friend / Marge Piercy / *147*

Housewife / Susan Fromberg Schaeffer / *147*

Homes of Single Women (excerpt) / Susan B. Anthony / *149*

The Second Sex (excerpt) / Simone de Beauvoir / *149*

Conversation with a Fireman from Brooklyn / Tess Gallagher / *149*

Clearing the Air / Nancy Willard / *150*

Farmwife / Betsy Sholl / *151*

The Victim / Ellen Bryant Voigt / *152*

Killers of the Dream (excerpt) / Lillian Smith / *153*

Adulthood / Nikki Giovanni / *153*
Watts (excerpt) / Shirley Kaufman / *155*
Yom Kippur / Chana Bloch / *155*

The Will toward the Good

To a Milkweed / Deborah Digges / *159*
Memoirs, I (excerpt) / Margaret Fuller / *159*
To Softness / Laurie Sheck / *160*
This Morning / Muriel Rukeyser / *161*
The Gardener / Robin Becker / *161*
The Woman with the Wild-Grown Hair Relaxes after Another Long Day / Nita Penfold / *162*
When he came (excerpt) / Dorothee Sölle / *163*
Prayer for a Tenspeed Heart / Barbara Hendryson / *164*
Aunt Jane of Kentucky (excerpt) / Eliza Calvert Hall / *164*
The Oven Loves the TV Set / Heather McHugh / *166*
3 : 6 (excerpt) / Alta / *167*
A Few Sirens / Alice Walker / *167*
The Network of the Imaginary Mother (excerpt) / Robin Morgan / *169*
Mother's Day Proclamation of 1870 / Julia Ward Howe / *169*
The low road / Marge Piercy / *170*
The seven of pentacles / Marge Piercy / *171*
To be of use / Marge Piercy / *172*
A just anger / Marge Piercy / *173*
It Is Dangerous to Read Newspapers / Margaret Atwood / *174*
Small Comfort / Katha Pollitt / *175*
Holy the Firm (excerpt) / Annie Dillard / *175*
Pilgrim at Tinker Creek (excerpt) / Annie Dillard / *176*
Eagle Poem / Joy Harjo / *176*
The Day Before They Bombed Nagasaki / Rebecca Baggett / *177*
Gathered at the River / Denise Levertov / *178*
Conspiracy / Claire Bateman / *180*
Our Passion for Justice (excerpt) / Carter Heyward / *181*
Beginners / Denise Levertov / *181*
The Fountain / Denise Levertov / *183*

Sacredness of the Ordinary

Matins (excerpt) / Denise Levertov / *187*
The Acolyte / Denise Levertov / *187*
Moon of the First Communion / Kathleen Norris / *188*
The Wedding in the Courthouse / Kathleen Norris / *189*
The Sky Is Full of Blue and Full of the Mind of God / Kathleen Norris / *190*
"Scientists find universe awash in tiny diamonds" / Pat Mayne Ellis / *191*

Salvation / George Ella Lyon / *192*
The Foot-Washing / George Ella Lyon / *193*
Nightingales in America / Jane Flanders / *194*
The Pedestrian Woman / Robin Morgan / *194*
Love Should Grow Up Like a Wild Iris in the Fields / Susan Griffin / *196*
Miracle / Susan Griffin / *197*
The Woman's Bible (excerpt) / Elizabeth Cady Stanton / *198*
how he is coming then / Lucille Clifton / *198*
Revolutionary Patience (excerpt) / Dorothee Sölle / *198*
Holy the Firm (excerpt) / Annie Dillard / *199*
Garlic / Jeanne Foster / *200*
Welcome Morning / Anne Sexton / *200*
domestic poem / Eileen Moeller / *201*
Beatitude / Claire Bateman / *202*
How to Stuff a Pepper / Nancy Willard / *202*

The Spirit and the Flesh Are One

Meditations with Julian of Norwich (excerpt) / Julian of Norwich / *207*
To praise / Ellen Bass / *207*
In Celebration of My Uterus / Anne Sexton / *208*
Use of the Erotic: The Erotic as Power (excerpt) / Audre Lorde / *210*
Revolutionary Patience (excerpt) / Dorothee Sölle / *211*
God send easter / Lucille Clifton / *212*
spring song / Lucille Clifton / *212*
The Network of the Imaginary Mother (excerpt) / Robin Morgan / *212*
Meditations with Hildegard of Bingen (excerpt) / Hildegard of Bingen / *213*
Saturday Night Worship / Ann Carhart / *214*
White Petticoats / Chana Bloch / *214*
O Taste and See / Denise Levertov / *215*
Common Prayer / Lynn Ungar / *216*
Catechism / Betsy Sholl / *217*
Sunrise / Mary Oliver / *218*
Adam Says See (excerpt) / Julia Randall / *219*

The Unity of All That Is

Our Houses / Linda Hogan / *223*
Subway / Susan Fawcett / *223*
Mrs. Schneider in Church / Kathleen Norris / *224*
Mass for the Day of St. Thomas Didymus (excerpt) / Denise Levertov / *225*
29. / Alta / *226*
The Way of All Ideology (excerpt) / Susan Griffin / *226*
The Sabbath of Mutual Respect / Marge Piercy / *227*
Chains of Fire (excerpt) / Elsa Gidlow / *230*

Dream 2: Brian the Still-Hunter / Margaret Atwood / *230*
cutting greens / Lucille Clifton / *231*
The House That Fear Built: Warsaw, 1943 / Jane Flanders / *231*
A Ceremony (excerpt) / Robin Morgan / *232*
Childhood of a Stranger / Claire Bateman / *233*
Dancing with Poets / Ellen Bryant Voigt / *233*
Remember / Joy Harjo / *234*
Untitled poem from "The Dinner Party" / Judy Chicago / *235*

Images of the Divine

Briefly It Enters, and Briefly Speaks / Jane Kenyon / *239*
The Bat / Jane Kenyon / *240*
Beyond God the Father (excerpt) / Mary Daly / *240*
Thank You, Lord (excerpt) / Maya Angelou / *241*
Sexism and God-Talk (excerpt) / Rosemary Ruether / *241*
Apotheosis of the Kitchen Goddess II / Teresa Noelle Roberts / *242*
They say she is veiled / Judy Grahn / *242*
When the Saints Come Marching In / Audre Lorde / *242*
October (excerpt) / Audre Lorde / *243*
The Spiral Dance (excerpt) / Starhawk / *244*
Nothing So Wise / Jeanne Lohmann / *244*
Meditations with Julian of Norwich (excerpt) / Julian of Norwich / *245*
Inventing Sin / George Ella Lyon / *245*
Teeth / Susan Griffin / *247*
Not So. Not So. / Anne Sexton / *247*
Woman's Call to the Ministry (excerpt) / Caroline Julia Bartlett / *248*
Nape / Jan Epton Seale / *249*
Kali / Lucille Clifton / *249*
Our Passion for Justice (excerpt) / Carter Heyward / *250*
In This Motherless Geography / Elaine Orr / *250*
for colored girls who have considered suicide when the rainbow is enuf (excerpt) / Ntozake
     Shange / *252*
Meditations with Hildegard of Bingen (excerpt) / Hildegard of Bingen / *252*
Resurrection / Margaret Atwood / *253*
Holy the Firm (excerpt) / Annie Dillard / *254*
Teaching a Stone to Talk (excerpt) / Annie Dillard / *255*
Epiphany / Pem Kremer / *255*
The Measure of My Days (excerpt) / Florida Scott-Maxwell / *256*
Eli, Eli / Miriam Kessler / *256*
The Color Purple (excerpt) / Alice Walker / *256*
Mass for the Day of St. Thomas Didymus (excerpt) / Denise Levertov / *257*
The Thread / Denise Levertov / *258*
The Task / Denise Levertov / *259*

The Tree / Cinda Thompson / 263
The Sacrifice / Chana Bloch / 263
Ruth / Diane Q. Lewis / 264
Lot's Wife / Cherra S. Ransom / 267
Job's Wife (excerpt) / Betsy Sholl / 267
Poem for Flora / Nikki Giovanni / 268
Delilah / Ellen Bryant Voigt / 269
Abishag / Shirley Kaufman / 270
the raising of lazarus / Lucille Clifton / 271
mary / Lucille Clifton / 271
holy night / Lucille Clifton / 272
Jesus Dies / Anne Sexton / 272
The Feast of the Assumption of the Virgin / Ellen Bryant Voigt / 273
to joan / Lucille Clifton / 274
Riding Hood / Betsy Sholl / 275
I and Thou / Chana Bloch / 276
The Two Gretels / Robin Morgan / 277
Myth / Muriel Rukeyser / 278
Maxim / Josephine Miles / 278
The Mermaid / Lisel Mueller / 279
ego-tripping (there may be a reason why) / Nikki Giovanni / 280
Everywoman Her Own Theology / Alicia Ostriker / 281

The Word

Why I Never Answered Your Letter / Nancy Willard / 285
Words & Language: A Haggle (excerpt) / Paula Gunn Allen / 285
tell our daughters / Besmilr Brigham / 286
Stories and Poems / Susan Griffin / 287
"Naming" from Woman and Nature / Susan Griffin / 287
Poem for a Chorus / Marie Cartier / 288
A Way of Staying Sane (excerpt) / Maxine Kumin / 289
The Last Class / Ellen Bryant Voigt / 290
the making of poems / Lucille Clifton / 291
One Writer's Beginnings (excerpt) / Eudora Welty / 291
Three Small Songs for the Muse / Kathleen Norris / 292
A Visit / George Ella Lyon / 293
She and the Muse / Denise Levertov / 295
The Secret / Denise Levertov / 296
'I learned that her name was Proverb.' / Denise Levertov / 297

Credits / 299
Index / 309

Preface

Let me begin with a story. About two years ago, I went to the beginning session of an adult education course called something like "Sources of Faith." It was led by one of the most deeply spiritual and inspired men that I know. He began by telling the group his assumptions and faith convictions. Throughout his presentation, he quoted from his teachers, from books, from the founders of Western thought—everyone from Aristotle to Auden—*and not once did he mention a woman's name or recall the words of a woman.* I went away feeling unacknowledged, nonexistent. How many women have had similar experiences in various institutions: schools, churches, places of work? The primary purpose of this book is to help right that overwhelming lack of balance in the public language that defines and articulates the parameters of our thinking and knowing.

Specifically, *Cries of the Spirit* addresses itself to the spiritual and the theological, the realm in which ultimate values are considered and claimed. Far from being peripheral to our existence, as the secular world of scientism and materialism might have us think, the realm of the spirit is in fact the essential, for what we claim as our god and what we conceive of as the good directs our every breath and every move. Spirituality has too long been an almost exclusively male realm, resting in abstract principle and institutionalized order. In contrast, women tend towards a relational sacrality that is based on the natural world of earth and flesh. The woman's perspective is healing and life-giving, one that we can ill afford to ignore.

I have conceived of a broad audience for this book, beginning with anyone who enjoys fine, moving poetry that addresses important life issues. The collection, however, should be of special interest to women who are claiming and redefining themselves in a culture that is just beginning to offer them a language in which to do that important work. It is a truism that the female gender has more often than not been stereotyped and trivialized in literature written by males. *Cries of the Spirit* is an anthology completely composed of women's words, a book in which female wisdom and power are honored. A woman reading this book will surely say with the poet Alta, "i'm a woman and i'm proud."

In addition, I offer this book as a resource for both male and female religious leaders and for lay-leaders, to use in whatever ways seem appropriate. I have long used poetry in the context of the worship service, either as part of the liturgy or within the sermon proper. Sometimes a single compelling metaphor from a poem can serve as the theme for a service. Readings may also work well as short meditation pieces, or to focus attention and create a mood at the beginning of a gathering, or to inspire at the close of a meeting or program. Women's literature—in particular the wealth of contemporary women's poetry—is strongly prophetic, and it is therefore invaluable to those of us who are about the business of awareness and redemption.

Many readers may have been alienated from their churches and synagogues, for these male-dominated institutions have been slow to recognize and incorporate a female consciousness. And yet the hungering for spiritual wholeness exists. I hope that *Cries of the Spirit* will provide a source of nourishment, life-giving bread for a new day, to those women who are exploring their spirituality, whether in traditional settings, in alternative church settings such as woman-church or Wicca, or simply in their own meditation and reflection.

I myself am a parish minister in a liberal denomination, the Unitarian Universalist, and in keeping with the principles of that faith, I set out to make this book inclusive of many religious traditions. I believe that I have done so: readers will find no particular institutional wash to the book, nor do I have any theological ax to grind. What, then, have been my principles of selection?

The readings that follow were chosen, first of all, because they reflect a vision of the sacred that seems to emerge from the particular consciousness of women. The work is embodied, earthy, relational. Female imagery and symbolism abound. I wanted every selection to breathe "woman."

Aesthetic quality was extremely important to me in my search. No matter how much I might have agreed with the sentiment of a particular piece, if it was not well crafted, I discarded it. Writing that I judged to be chiefly propaganda, leaning heavily on rhetoric, was also passed by.

The pieces included here are not typically "liturgical" in the sense of being appropriate only for ritual. Language of ritual too often degenerates into lofty abstractions, carried only by the accoutrements of the occasion. I tried to choose pieces that can stand alone, and stand over a period of time, as fine pieces of writing.

On the other hand, I chose pieces that are readily accessible in a single reading, so that they may be used for public occasions. Some poets, including many excellent ones—Emily Dickinson, for example—do not lend themselves to my particular purposes, because of the subtlety and even profundity of their work. Length was a consideration, too. Long selections have to be very compelling to command attention when read to a group, so I gravitated toward shorter pieces with single, clear themes.

The overwhelming majority of the writers I chose are contemporary American poets and writers. I did, however, dip into the past and into some translated work because I found certain pieces—such as the quotation from Simone de Beauvoir—to be powerfully relevant to our times. The work of Hildegard of Bingen and Julian of Norwich has attracted new interest because of recent retranslations and seems amazingly contemporary, though it was written hundreds of years ago.

I freely admit that my own prejudices were operating during the long process: like any editor, I chose what I liked, what moved me. In particular, I looked for passion, for integrity, for compassion, for commitment to the greater good, in the writers I chose. I looked for flesh and feeling.

My research was inductive. I didn't start with feminist aesthetic theory nor with any preconceived ideas about typology. Theory and typology came later, after I had sifted through thousands of poems to see what women are saying and how they are saying it. Certain themes kept coming up repeatedly, and I began to see patterns emerge. About three-quarters of the way through the process of collecting, I decided on the titles designating the emphases of the various sections. Sometimes I found it difficult to know which section would best suit a particular piece, for there is much overlapping of theme and subject matter. My quandary supports my contention that there is, in fact, a female aesthetic of the sacred that is clear and identifiable.

Some of the pieces in this collection will not suit certain groups or occasions. The direct, earthy language in one poem might make it just right to open a session of a women's support group, but inappropriate for a Sunday morning worship service (though I believe that it is the responsibility of religious leaders to "stretch" congregants' notions of acceptable language for services, lest we prettify ourselves into irrelevance). Often I find that a few words of introduction, calling attention to the major theme of a poem, allow the listeners easier access.

As this project winds to a close, I'm finding myself reluctant to stop. I have received tremendous pleasure from the seeking, sometimes sitting at my kitchen table in tears over a particular poem, or laughing out loud with the pleasure of identification. I've discovered new poets or little-known poets— and part of the joy of this book is in introducing them to you. And personally I have been blessed by immersing myself so completely for two years in the wisdom, courage, and love of these women's words. I have received more than I could ever give. Now I pass these words on to you, in love. May you be blessed in turn, as I have been.

Acknowledgments

I am most grateful to the Grants Panel of the Unitarian Universalist Association for the financial help in securing permissions for reprinting of published pieces in *Cries of the Spirit*. Bill Schulz, president of the UUA, is due special thanks for his encouragement during the early stages of the book, as is Joan Kahn-Schneider.

During much of the selection process, I was guided by an advisory board from the Pacific Central District of the UUA. Those serving on the board included Astri Birbach, worship chair of the U.U. Fellowship of Napa-Solano; Johanna Nichols-Marcus, minister of the First Universalist Church of Auburn, Maine; Jann Rose Schaub, worship chair of the Mt. Diablo Unitarian Universalist Church; Liz Fisher, co-facilitator of the Women and Religion Task Force of the Pacific Central District; Til Evans, acting president of Starr King School for the Ministry; and chair, Jeanne Foster, teacher at St. Mary's College in Moraga, California. Jeanne deserves special mention because she continued to give me counsel and support long after the Board had ceased its official functioning, in particular by discussing with me the quality and appropriateness of individual pieces.

I owe a debt of gratitude to the many persons who suggested specific readings for *Cries of the Spirit*: Barbara Bush, Mark Belletini, Elizabeth Green, Margo Gross, Robbie Cranch, Helene Knox, Dennis Hamilton, Jeanne Foster, Harry Scholefield, Kathleen Norris, Jann Rose Schaub, Paul Sawyer, Betsy Sholl, Janine Canan, Beverly Smrha, Gordon McKeeman, and others too numerous to mention. Beverly Smrha remains strongly in my memory as the first person to whom I spoke about my idea for such an anthology. Her smile and enthusiastic encouragement did much to get me on my way.

Reaching back to the past, I wish to thank Wendell Berry, who first taught me the power and preciousness of words. George Ella Lyon has encouraged me in my writing for long years, and never lost faith that this book would be born. She provided valuable suggestions in the final stages of revising the introduction to this volume. Susan Griffin lent her wisdom and support at several crucial points in the process of completing *Cries*.

My editor at Beacon Press, Deborah Johnson, is due thanks for her patient support and helpful concrete suggestions. Dawn Ace, my assistant in securing permissions, showed devoted persistence in her efforts.

Most particularly, I wish to express my love and appreciation for Clare

Benedicks Fischer, Aurelia Henry Rhinehardt Professor of Religion and Culture at Starr King School for the Ministry. As my teacher, mentor, and friend, Clare has given of herself unstintingly, not only rendering superb guidance, but genuinely helping me to *become*—to believe in myself and in my work. For this, I shall ever be grateful.

Introduction

*When I write, it's everything that we don't know we can be that is
written out of me, without exclusions, without stipulation, and
everything we will be calls us to the unflagging, intoxicating,
unappeasable search for love. In one another we will never be lacking.*
—Hélène Cixous

Not long ago I discovered that I have no language. Not just me personally, of
course, but women. Women have no language.

That discovery shook me deeply. It explained perhaps why I often have
this sense of muteness, this pulling back from known words and patterns of
language, this doubling back and redoubling upon myself. But where am I to
find a voice? The cultural/lingual patterns were laid in place, solidly, years
before I even came into this world, were they not?

All writers must be creators, but women writers must create twice: we
must re-create our materials—the very words and word-patterns of our me-
dium—and at the same time we must create our individual pieces of writing.
We have no ready-made system, no vocabulary in place, no easy syntax, no
context of allusion, no given subject matter to embrace us and call us forth.

Where can we begin? Perhaps with the silences, the monumental silences: the multitude of feelings and understandings that we have discounted
as not real because there has arisen no word, no phrase, no pattern of thinking
to legitimate our experience. To remain in these silences is to be alone. There
is no way to connect flesh with flesh, no way to perceive, to preserve, to *know*.
So we fumble with words, playing with them, caressing them, trying to tease
out meaning. We work as if our lives were at stake. As if *life* were at stake. And
we would be right in supposing so.

Hear the words of Monique Wittig in *Les guérillères*:

> The women say, the language you speak poisons your glottis
> tongue palate lips. They say, the language you speak is made up of
> words that are killing you. They say, the language you speak is made
> up of signs that rightly speaking designate what men have appropri-
> ated. Whatever they have not laid hands on, whatever they have not
> pounced on like many-eyed birds of prey, does not appear in the lan-
> guage you speak. This is apparent precisely in the *intervals* that your

masters have not been able to *fill* with their words of proprietors and possessors, this can be found in the *gaps*, in all which is not a continuation of their discourse, in the zero, the o, the perfect circle that you invent to imprison them and to overthrow them.[1]

Cries of the Spirit speaks to the silences, the intervals, the gaps—it honors the "perfect circle" of Wittig. Most of the book is composed of works by contemporary poets, women writing after 1960. Though there were experimental poets before that time (consider Gertrude Stein, Mina Loy, H. D., for example), it remained for the political and social climate of the sixties to allow so many female poets to challenge convention in such daring and open ways, their work pouring forth in an unprecedented flood of energy and experimentation.

Anne Sexton and Sylvia Plath were among the first, of course, and they suffered mightily for their difference. Later came Susan Griffin and Alta and Alice Walker and June Jordan and Adrienne Rich and Marge Piercy and on and on and on. They knew that they were part of a larger social revolution— one in which women acted to support other women, instead of seeing them as rivals for the attentions of men—and in that community of strength and mutuality, they dared to shake the establishment. They began creating a language to embody their experience. They began writing about subject matter that came directly from their lives—clean towels and tea kettles; menstruation and abortion and pregnancy and childbirth; love and friendship; the preparation of food; the protection of the very old and the very young; death and loss and the continuing of generations. They wrote openly of their fears and their angers, instead of hinting at or suggesting them, as their precursors had often done. They laid claim to their lives.

But the revolution did not stop with the personal. "What would happen if one woman told the truth about her life? / The world would split open," wrote Muriel Rukeyser. Fierce poems of social protest—poems about racism and poverty and war—arose to stand beside poems about home and family: the body and the body politic were one. Owning the pain and disintegration that are inevitably a part of transformation, these writers gave themselves to change.

Cries of the Spirit, then, falls within the larger literary picture of what has happened with contemporary women's poetry,[2] and it should be seen in that context. However, this book makes still another assertion: I believe that much of women's poetry today could properly be described as prophetic. That is, it shows us where we as a culture have gone astray spiritually. Through a powerful female aesthetic, it redefines and clarifies the sacred and calls us back home.

But what do I mean when I use the word *sacred?* Traditionally, the sacred has meant something consecrated or set apart as holy. It is connected with religious rites or ritual. In other words, the sacred has to do with organization and order. It has to do with institution. It is baptism, not birthing, for example. It is the public ceremony of marriage, not the private ceremony of

making love. For redefinition, I was thrown back to myself, to my inner knowing and the knowing of the women whose words I had immersed myself in for
two years.

Virtually all of the writers included in this volume would probably consider themselves secular, in that they are not particularly interested in writing
for religious reasons per se. And yet when I read their work, I find that I am
moved toward wholeness. *That which moves toward wholeness.* That's part of my
definition of the sacred.

"But doesn't art universally perform this function?" you may counter.
Some does, surely. And yet much of modern art has to do with disintegration
and hopelessness. Though a particular work may be aesthetically satisfying,
the reader or viewer or listener often goes away with a sense of emptiness or
even despair. "It's great," I heard someone say of a large collage at a recent art
opening, "but I would hate to hang it on my wall and look at it every day."

In contrast, I find that contemporary women's poetry largely speaks of
life and hope. Even the poetry that focuses on the alienation and violence of
modern life does so in a prophetic voice that by implication urges us to turn
from our present ways, lest we perish. Perhaps—and there's no way of knowing if I'm correct—women's intimate connection with the flesh, with creating
and sustaining life, brings forth these impulses in their writing.

The sacred also has to do, I think, with thankfulness, that most basic of
religious impulses. Thankfulness for being alive, for the wonder of our bodies:
for being able to breathe and eat and drink and walk about and make love. It
has to do most profoundly with acknowledging connection, with knowing
that there is really no such thing as autonomy, for we are all one with the
other. The sacred is not in the sky, the place of transcendent, abstract principle, but rather is based on this earth, in the ordinary dwelling places of our
lives, in our gardens and kitchens and bedrooms. And it is no less present in
our places of protest, the streets and public halls and institutions where we
express our outrage at the reckless squandering of the life that is one. The
sacred is fueled by eros, by desire. It is about passion. And compassion. And
love. Always love. Love over and over and over again, love.

For women, the sacred seems to be rooted in experience, rather than in
institution—in the body and in nature, not in culture.[3] Institutional language
narrows and constrains, but experience elbows its way out, to a broader
place. Poetry is its natural vehicle. Who can order the Holy? It is like a rain
forest, dripping, lush, fecund, wild. We enter its abundance at our peril, for
here we are called to the wholeness for which we long, but which requires all
we are and can hope to be.

THE ONENESS OF SPIRIT AND FLESH

Women's poetry starts with the body. Their writing refuses the separation of
matter and spirit, the philosophical status quo in Western culture. Women do

not see the body as the subversive vessel of the sacred, but as one with the sacred, a stance that obviously makes it harder to offer flesh so casually on the altar of principle.

Such a bold embracing of spirit and flesh is clear in Anne Sexton's "In Praise of My Uterus," a poem some would still find shocking:

> Sweet weight,
> in celebration of the woman I am
> and of the soul of the woman I am
> and of the central creature and its delight
> I sing for you. I dare to live.
> Hello, spirit. Hello, cup.
> Fasten, cover. Cover that does contain.
> Hello to the soil of the fields.
> Welcome, roots.

In women's poetry, the sexual relationship is transformed: it is not presented as a power struggle in which one partner tries to dominate the other, but rather as a hunger for and a movement toward closeness, an intimacy of body and spirit in ecstatic union. Sex is not about conquest, but about invitation and reception and renewal. Linda Hogan ends her poem "A Thought" with the following words:

> But can't we swallow the sweetness
> and can't you sing in my arms
> and sleep in the human light
> of the sun and moon I have been
> drinking alone.
> Later we will rise up
> and shake the sleep from our arms
> and find we were not broken down
> at all.

Our cultural split between spirit and matter has rendered the lie that flesh is to be feared and avoided. We are obsessed with controlling our bodies so that they—terrible, mortal things that they are—will not control us. We relentlessly lose weight (again and again), we jog, we firm, we tone. When the flesh goes flabby, after all, we can never be loved. And that quivering body is the sure evidence that death is on the way. Says Erica Jong in her poem "Aging":

> the belly may be kept firm through numerous pregnancies
> by means of sit-ups jogging dancing (think of Russian ballerinas)
>   & the cunt
> as far as I know is ageless possibly immortal becoming simply
> more open more quick to understand more dry-eyed than at 22

>   which

after all is what you were dying for (as you ravaged
islands of turtles beehives oystersbeds the udders of cows)
desperate to censor changes which you simply might have let play
over you lying back listening opening yourself
      letting the years make love the only way
        (poor blunders)

           they know

In contrast to its traditional role as a reminder of death, the flesh in women's writings returns to the natural world as source, sacredness, fertility, connection, unity. The body, as the French feminists would say, is *jouissance,* or joy.

Such fleshly writing is subversive of the order of things. The body has its own way of knowing, a knowing that has little to do with logic, and much to do with truth; little to do with control, and much to do with acceptance; little to do with division and analysis, and much to do with union.

Don't mistake the danger here—the body is hated and rejected in this culture, mainly in deeply unconscious ways. All our elaborate and worshipful care of it is not love, but helpless anger and fear. "You couldn't use these poems in my church," said one woman to me during a workshop.

"Why not?" I asked.

"They're too—*intense,*" she answered.

Truth tends to shake us to our very bones. For God's sake, what should the church be about?

METAPHOR FROM THE NATURAL WORLD

Female metaphor rests in the natural world: water, earth, seed, moon: circles and more circles, cycles of dying and beginning anew, the endless coming round of generations. This kind of figurative language appears in Kathleen Norris's poem "Advent," which acknowledges the sacredness of pregnancy. Pregnant women are seen as part of the natural world of regeneration and fecundity: they are "fruit," "ripening melons," "like a ripe papaya." They are connected with the power of wind and wildness and the sea. Participating willingly, carefully, in the great cycles of existence, "They are home / and exile, beginning and end, / end and means." Pregnant women are the protectors of us all, for they "part the sea / and pass down the bloody length of it." As the poet listens, "the holy wind breathes through them."

Pregnancy, birth, and mothering are no longer overlooked as insignificant subjects, the way they have been traditionally. What could be more sacred than the bringing forth of life? Since women are honoring their bodies as part of the sacredness of the natural world, it follows that they draw much of their imagery and figurative language from these sources.

Of course, if one conceives of nature as something to be conquered and used for one's own purposes—the prevailing message from our own Judeo-Christian culture—then identifying woman with nature is tantamount to denigrating her. But in these women's poems, there is awe, mystery, and primal power, not fear and denigration. No more disembodied Virgin. No more lady on the pedestal, unreachable. Here is woman, giver of life.

SOURCE OF AUTHORITY WITHIN THE WRITER

Women have gone within themselves to find their own sources of spiritual truth. We didn't have much of an alternative, really. Where were we to go for meaning, for identity? To books written with the assumption that the male perspective is also the human perspective? To the arts, where woman is pictured as madonna, virgin, or whore? To the mass media, where she is seen as an object for consumption?

The female poet has chosen to explore her daily experience, the realities of her life: she writes about the shape of her body—as it is, not as it has been worshiped and despised—about sexual loving, about childbirth, about abortion. She writes of household rituals, the caretaking that keeps life going. She writes of her pain and longings, her experiences of oppression. She often makes the connection between her personal, inner experience and her understanding of the systemic injustice which institutionalizes and perpetuates that oppression. She is often angry, sometimes vengeful, but she tries to emerge from the ruckus clear-sighted and whole, her "no" leading to her "yes."

She writes consistently, tenaciously, about relationship. "Love should grow like a wild iris," says Susan Griffin, "but does not."

> Love more often is to be found in kitchens at the dinner hour,
> tired out and hungry, lingers over tables in houses where
> the walls record movements; while the cook is probably angry,
> and the ingredients of the meal are budgeted, while some
> where a child cries feed me now and her mother not quite
> hysterical says over and over, wait just a bit, just a bit,
> love should grow up in the fields like a wild iris
> but never does

George Ella Lyon writes eloquently about the messy details of childbirth, yielding up a sacred event connected irrevocably with the erotic.[4]

> As you wailed in your heated bed
> a nurse held the pan so I could see
> that valentine we all arrive with,
> that red pad of which you were the lily
> with the cord lying bleached across it
> like a root pulled from the water
> like a heartroot torn free.

What is to be honored? Where does value lie? We have all been taught that the order of things—whether in the home or in the nation or in the world—is a ladder given to us by God and Darwin, a ladder not to be questioned, and that violence is the way to handle disorder in the hierarchy. Could it be that another way might be found, a way more in keeping with justice and the continuity of life? Women's concerns and women's ways of knowing move us toward the wholeness we long for in the midst of the fragmentation we feel.

EMPHASIS ON FEELING

Cutting across time and culture, women's literature has always emphasized feeling. In the nineteenth century in our country—with the notable exception of the poetic genius of Emily Dickinson—feeling in women's poetry fell into a sticky goo of sentimentality. Sentimentality comes from an inability, for whatever reason, to look reality in the face. For its power, it depends on the stock response. The feelings expressed, then, are *derived* ones, feelings not authentically based within the writer. But today "personal" poetry is newly defined, and the feeling expressed in contemporary female writing is anything but sentimental. Feeling has been transformed into an expression of the life force, or erotic power, within the writer.

In women's writing, that power of feeling sometimes presents itself as a raging rejection of injustice, as in "A Just Anger," by Marge Piercy:

> Anger shines through me.
> Anger shines through me.
> I am a burning bush.
> My rage is a cloud of flame.
> My rage is a cloud of flame
> in which I walk
> seeking justice
> like a precipice.

There are exquisite love poems as well, not poems of frailty and dependence, but rather poetry that tells of a longing for a union that brings life and wholeness, a union of equals. Mary Oliver's beautiful lyric poem "Blossom" is exemplary:

> . . . when the burning
>   begins the most
> thoughtful among us dreams
>   of hurrying down
>   into the black petals,
>   into the fire,
> into the night where time lies shattered,
> into the body of another.

Female poets exhort us, over and over again, to love: without love, they say, we are lost. It is our only hope, personal or global. In Tess Gallagher's "The Hug," she tells of hugging a homeless man, and implies that we are all looking for a place of belonging:

> Clearly, a little permission is a dangerous thing.
> But when you hug someone you want it
> to be a masterpiece of connection, the way the button
> on his coat will leave the imprint of
> a planet in my cheek
> when I walk away. When I try to find some place
> to go back to.

To honor feeling is in itself prophetic, in a cultural system that glorifies the "rational" and the scientific as the sole authors of our salvation while we plunge headlong toward hell. Women's poetry most often exists to *move* us, not to entertain us with clever use of language, nor to explore abstract philosophical positions. It is a way to the heart. It opens the door to the spirit.

THE IMPERATIVE OF INTIMACY

There is an "imperative of intimacy" in women's poetry, says Alicia Ostriker.[5] The persona of the poem is usually the poet, being there with the reader, sharing the details of a life as if over coffee, identifying, making connection.

In "New Mother," by Sharon Olds, the poet shares a very intimate moment with the reader as she tells of her husband's tenderness after the birth of their child. But the moment is hardly confined to her experience alone, for she reminds us of the character of love itself:

> all of you so tender, you hung over me,
> over the nest of stitches,
> over the splitting and tearing, with the patience of someone who
> finds a wounded animal in the woods
> and stays with it, not leaving its side
> until it is whole, until it can run again.

In contemporary women's poetry, strength and joy often shine through. And yet these feelings do not emerge so much from individual questing and conquering as from the pleasures and satisfactions of relationship: lovemaking, friendships, partnerships, kinship. Here we have a radical challenge to the warrior hero in his lonely quest for the holy grail. Here the longing is for the falling down of barriers, the healing of division.

Joyce Carol Oates ends her poem "Growing Together" with the following words:

rising, pulling back my long sweaty hair
I see a face in the mirror only half mine
what I am thinking is only half mine
these words are only half mine
the frayed threads of our bodies want
only that tangling again
that old growing together again
a completion like the exhaling
of a single breath

Trust cannot be given carelessly, for there is much woundedness about, and those who have been betrayed often betray in turn. And yet there are people of honor and places of refuge. One might well ask, what is the alternative to trust? Have we not had isolation enough? Recognizing our longing for closeness, our need for nearness, is not weakness but wisdom.

DIRECT, HONEST LANGUAGE

The form of contemporary women's poetry is consistent with the movement toward closeness in that the writing is open, loose, informal, often conversational. It can be playful or even ribald. It is language that for the most part ignores allusion to the literary canon and revels instead in common speech, heart-talk. It is of-the earth.

For example, Nikki Giovanni could be sitting across your breakfast table as she speaks of her childhood in "Nikki-Rosa":

And though you're poor it isn't poverty that
concerns you
and though they fought a lot
it isn't your father's drinking that makes any difference
but only that everybody is together and you
and your sister have happy birthdays and very good
Christmasses

It is as if the old forms had to be cracked open before the new could emerge. The poetry often strikes one as stripped clean or even raw. There is no room for self-conscious cleverness or display of ego, which create distance; rather, here is language that yearns to reveal, to lay bare. The language is not adornment, but essence.

This direct style, mimicking daily patterns of speech, breaks the ladders of hierarchy. Sometimes only lower-case letters are used; punctuation may resemble that used in a note to an intimate. Examples abound, including the poetry of Lucille Clifton (who writes in the Black vernacular), Anne Sexton, Alice Walker, Marge Piercy, Kathleen Fraser, and, most particularly, Alta.

Alta is the preeminent poet who springs to mind when I think of honest, bare language. She reaches my heart through her very ingenuousness and boldness, in both language and subject matter. In her poem "104." from *Shameless Hussy*, she writes about a forbidden topic, miscarriage:

> what shall i wear
> to suffer my third miscarriage?
> something appealing but not sexy.
> i never want to look sexy anymore;
> not if i have to step outside my home.
>
> (for the visit to the doctor
> i wore a red skirt / blood
> on blood-red, who would notice?
> & tucked my shirt in, to reveal
> my fetchingly flat belly /
> but everyone knew i was bleeding
> anyway, the tears wouldn't stop.)

Conversational, almost painfully open, she invites the reader into her personal thought process as she contemplates "what shall i wear," when the question has become meaningless because of the depth of her pain and loss.

Although Alta is perhaps the most extreme practitioner of direct, honest language, this approach is pervasive in contemporary women's writing. It is suited for language of the spirit because it breaks down emotional barriers and opens the reader to the stirrings of the heart. It prepares a place.

OWNING OF SELF

One of the interesting and gratifying changes in women's writing since the 1960s is women's reluctance to play the role of victim, a position that cripples pride and denies power. Lucille Iverson ends her poem "Outrage" by refusing the male definition of woman and replacing it with an insistence on her own empowering vision:

> My Passion is
> Mine, nor am I
> Vampire, nor
> Banshee, nor
> Screamer, nor
> Waiting;   —I
> Have turned away, and   I
> Face a distance I
> Have not run;   —I
> Raise my fist beside the

Door of My Dreams and I
Take Time,
My Time,
All of it
In my Hands.

The paradox is that in order to come close, we must have the capacity to choose distance. In a poem that tells of relationship between equals, "To Have without Holding," Marge Piercy says we must neither own nor be owned:

Learning to love differently is hard,
love with the hands wide open, love
with the doors banging on their hinges,
the cupboard unlocked, the wind
roaring and whimpering in the rooms
rustling the sheets and snapping the blinds
that thwack like rubber bands
in an open palm.

We women have been taught to please everybody but ourselves and our God. Demigods are all around, including in church and synagogue, demanding that we do their bidding. But in order to come fully to the encounter with whatever gives ultimate meaning, in order to really wrestle with the angel, one must be a free agent, not defined by another, or by cultural imperatives. We acknowledge connection, we own bondedness as a good. Self-sacrifice is still possible and can be spiritually ennobling—but we must choose our own kneeling places and not have thrust upon us an agenda foreign to our spirits.

Women's poetry, speaking powerfully from the integrity of self-ownership, helps give us the courage to align ourselves with the Holy, at the center, in the splendor of our strength and wisdom. It is the only choice worth making.

THE UNITY OF ALL LIFE

Much of women's poetry bears witness to the essential unity that underlies all things. The physicists are right, in fact, when they explain to us that separation is an illusion, something the mystics of various traditions have known for hundreds of years. Native American poet Linda Hogan speaks for this kind of oneness in her poem "Our Houses":

Neighbors, the old woman who knows you
turns over in me
and I wake up
another country. There's no more
north and south.

Asleep, we pass through one another
like blowing snow,
all of us,
all.

And Lucille Clifton says, speaking of the simple act of preparing greens for dinner, "the greens roll black under the knife, / and the kitchen twists dark on its spine / and i taste in my natural appetite / the bond of live things everywhere." All that lives, all that is, of that I am a part.

CENTRALITY OF RELATIONSHIP

The understanding of our primal unity makes relationship a central concept in female identity and in women's literature. Because females apparently have a more fluid sense of ego boundaries than do males, there is danger that a woman may become "confluent," submerged in the needs of others, and lose all sense of self. And yet, to know that we are one with one another, that the nature of the universe is unity, that even material boundaries are illusory, seems a positive reference point in a society in which, sadly, alienation has become the norm.

Autonomy, independence? These are the cultural fantasies of a people who attempt to control matter and try to conquer even death. We are dependent every moment of every day upon one another—for our daily bread, for example, and that's only the beginning. Women's writing draws us to the reality of our connectedness and therefore to the possibility of community. Writes Claire Bateman in her poem "Childhood of a Stranger":

there is a debt between us even now
that our autonomy cannot remove:
a bent toward something more than tolerance,
older than kindness, oddly akin to love.

Our warrior-heroes of the past who conquered with the sword may need to give way to a new figure: one who takes the risks, not of physical danger but of loving deeply and devotedly; one who has, instead of a great capacity for harming, a great capacity for healing. Our weapons have given us no room for winning in the conventional sense. We must find a way to live together, if we are to live at all.

PROPHETIC VOICE FOR JUSTICE

Moral and political commitment is evident in much of contemporary women's poetry. In the hands of lesser writers, a very direct addressing of political issues can degenerate into mere propaganda, and then artistic value is greatly diminished. But when the writer is able to hold an aesthetic perspective, a

powerful, universal evocation can result, as it does in Denise Levertov's "The
Fountain":

> Don't say, don't say there is no water.
> That fountain is there among its scalloped
> green and gray stones,
> it is still there and always there
> with its quiet song and strange power
> to spring in us,
> up and out through the rock.

Marge Piercy is acutely sensitive to issues of justice, and many of her poems call the reader to awareness and action. In "The woman in the ordinary," the freshness of the poet's imagery and her cutting honesty make her words invigorating and inspiring:

> The woman of the golden fleece
> laughs uproariously from the belly
> inside the girl who imitates
> a Christmas card virgin with glued hands,
> who fishes for herself in other's eyes,
> who stoops and creeps to make herself smaller.
> In her bottled up is a woman peppery as curry,
> a yam of a woman of butter and brass,
> compounded of acid and sweet like a pineapple,
> like a handgrenade set to explode,
> like goldenrod ready to bloom.

Women write fiercely and prophetically of their own pain and anger, but they often seem acutely sensitive to the pain of other oppressed groups as well. Women's literature, along with other minority literature, has helped fill the silences with truth-telling of the poor and disenfranchised. Alice Walker asks in her poem "A Few Sirens,"

> wasn't there a time
> when food was sacred?
>
> When a dead child
> starved naked
> among the oranges
> in the marketplace
> spoiled
> the appetite?

Spirituality does not thrive in a vacuum: love, the fruit of the spirit, cannot help speaking in a prophetic voice, cannot help asserting itself in prophetic deeds. In the words of women, we come to understand that there is no such thing as individual redemption, that wholeness in our own lives is inevitably tied to the well-being of the rest of creation, including and most particularly the ones who have been set aside as "other" because of their skin color or class or national origin or sexual orientation or frailty of mind or body. Whatever offends the dignity of my brother or sister offends me. And my brothers and sisters are everywhere.

REVISING THE CULTURAL MYTHS

How well we know the stories we live by! Snow White, waiting for her prince. Mary, the mother of God, perpetual virgin. Eve, who brought sin and death into the world. Religious mythology is particularly dangerous, for it permeates all of Western art and literature, provides allusion for common speech, guides the ethical systems out of which much of our law emerges.

Realizing that our cultural mythology is so often degrading for women, female writers are bent on telling the stories anew, this time from a different perspective. (Elizabeth Cady Stanton, who supervised the translation of *The Woman's Bible,* is a striking early example of this movement.) These revisionist poems often seem amusing, for the reader is taken aback by the fresh approach, which reveals the hidden assumptions in the text. Sometimes the poetry seems irreverent—and it is, because of the cultural reverence we give to traditional mythos. Powerful images live in the stories that have been repeated to us since we were small: their truth seems as real as the touch of our mother's hand, as tangible as the back door that we slammed over and over as we went out to play. But these stories, after all, were created out of a consciousness emerging from a particular cultural milieu at a particular time in history. They are not TRUTH, and we should not treat them as such. Revising them can be revealing and empowering for women.

Murial Rukeyser has some fun with the Oedipus story in her playful but pointed poem "Myth":

> Long afterward, Oedipus, old and blinded, walked the
> roads.   He smelled a familiar smell.   It was
> the Sphinx.   Oedipus said, "I want to ask one question.
> Why didn't I recognize my mother?"   "You gave the
> wrong answer," said the Sphinx.   "But that was what
> made everything possible," said Oedipus.   "No," she said.
> "When I asked, What walks on four legs in the morning,
> two at noon, and three in the evening, you answered,
> Man.   You didn't say anything about woman."
> "When you say Man," said Oedipus, "you include women
> too. Everyone knows that."   She said, "That's what
> you think."

Betsy Sholl fleshes out the picture of the Biblical figure known to us only as "Job's wife" in her poem of the same title. Job's wife addresses God, unashamedly admitting that she has told Job to "curse God and die":

So you're God.
Tell me I'm straw, chaff, mist.

Tell me the sea has springs
deep and cold as dreams
that make me wake exhausted.

Enough thunder.
What have you done
with my children?

We dare not let ourselves be unconsciously defined by a mythology that shows women to be dependent, subservient, evil, and less than fully human. Challenging the canon in outrageous ways brings into relief those patterns that have told us we are less than we are and allows us to suggest different patterns, stories with bold, new endings.

RE-VISIONING THE DIVINE

The revisionist movement is nowhere clearer than when women write of the Divine. God is almost always seen as immanent, not as an abstract, transcendent being "above" the earth. God is incarnated, made manifest in the flesh, present most fully in *relationship*. "I am food on the prisoner's plate . . . / I am water rushing to the wellhead, / filling the pitcher until it spills," writes Jane Kenyon.

Denise Levertov, in her magnificent "Mass for the Day of St. Thomas Didymus," pictures a vulnerable God very different from the omnipotent figure of traditional religion: "is it implied that *we* must protect this perversely weak / animal, whose muzzle's nudgings / suppose there is milk to be found in us?"

Given the new sense of pride in self, plus historical research into Goddess figures, many women inevitably are moved to see God in female images. "Let God come like a thick dumb mother cat, / pick up what's left by the nape of its neck, / and move it to safe quarters," writes Jan Epton Seale, as she characterizes what death might be like for her. George Ella Lyon gives us an angry Goddess/mother figure who does not look kindly on the mess we've made of things:

God is fed up
All the oceans she gave us
All the fields
All the acres of steep seedful forests
And we did what
     Invented the Great Chain
         of Being and
       the chain saw
    Invented sin

Hebrew scripture says that man was made in the image of God, but the converse also appears to be true: God was made in the image of man—Michelangelo's fearsome old white-bearded patriarch reaching down his arm to the newly created Adam. Now, after centuries of forgetfulness, God may once again be made in the image of woman, as well—one who receives, who holds and protects, who brings forth life. The metaphors by which we embrace the mysteries beyond our knowing are becoming inclusive of women's experience.

CONCLUSION

A revolution has started, there's no doubt about it. And what will happen if the masculine world order, built on language, continues to be challenged and shaken? "Then all the stories would have to be told differently," writes Hélène Cixous, "the future would be incalculable, the historical forces would, will, change hands, bodies, another thinking as yet not thinkable, will transform the functioning of all society."[6]

Can we not envision a world in which both men and women honor the flesh, refusing to separate it from spirit, cherishing the earthly as holy stuff? Can we not envision a time when caring for and nurturing both the earth and one another become more important than dominating and conquering? Can we not look forward to the day when we regard all living things as part of the creative matrix, from which we cannot divorce ourselves and survive?

I am not a separatist: I do not conceive of men, or a particular man, as the enemy. But the entrenched system of patriarchy is death-dealing, and in contrast to the stench of decay all about, women choose to write of life. I see it everywhere I turn in their work. I suppose the reverse of Professor Higgins' question haunts me: "Why can't a man be more like a woman?" Not that it is our job to save him—but all who are privileged and burdened to live just now do have some responsibility for creating a world that is safer and saner and more just than the one we have. What better way to do it than with words, holy words.

NOTES

1. Monique Wittig, *Les guérillères*, trans. David LeVay (New York: Viking Press, 1971). Quoted by Xavière Gauthier in "Creations," *New French Feminisms*, ed. Elaine Marks and Isabelle de Courtivron (New York: Schocken Books, 1981), 163. (Italics are Xavière Gauthier's.)

2. For a thorough and beautifully written analysis of this subject matter, see Alicia Ostriker, *Stealing the Language: The Emergence of Women's Poetry in America* (Boston: Beacon Press, 1986).

3. This is not to say that the sacred cannot be evoked in cultural institutions such as churches and synagogues, but it cannot be imposed from there, which is a different matter.

4. I use the word *erotic* here and elsewhere as Audre Lorde speaks of it: "*eros*, the personification of love in all its aspects . . . an assertion of the life force." In Lorde, "Uses of

the Erotic: The Erotic as Power" (Trumansberg, New York: Out and Out Books, 1978), p. 3
of unnumbered text.

5. Ostriker, *Stealing the Language*, 166.

6. Hélène Cixous, "Sorties," *La jeune née*, trans. Ann Liddle (Paris: Union Générale d'Editions, 10/18, 1975). Cited in Alicia Ostriker, "The Thieves of Language," in *Writing Like a Woman* (Ann Arbor: The University of Michigan Press, 1983).

Owning Self

Traditionally, a woman's life was not her own: she belonged first to daddy and then to husband. Indeed, she was raised with the expectation that she would be—literally, body and soul—somebody else's. Today, women are claiming their lives. We still choose love and intimate relationship, but not as reasons for being. We can no longer live through others. In the following selections, the reader will sense the exhilaration of women as they allow themselves the freedom to discover their strengths, accept their power, and make choices out of the integrity of their deepest spiritual impulses.

Unlearning to not Speak
Marge Piercy

Blizzards of paper
in slow motion
sift through her.
In nightmares she suddenly recalls
a class she signed up for
but forgot to attend.
Now it is too late.
Now it is time for finals:
losers will be shot.
Phrases of men who lectured her
drift and rustle in piles:
Why don't you speak up?
Why are you shouting?
You have the wrong answer,
wrong line, wrong face.
They tell her she is womb-man,
babymachine, mirror image, toy,
earth mother and penis-poor,
a dish of synthetic strawberry icecream
rapidly melting.
She grunts to a halt.
She must learn again to speak
starting with I
Starting with We
starting as the infant does
with her own true hunger
and pleasure
and rage.

The woman in the ordinary
Marge Piercy

The woman in the ordinary pudgy downcast girl
is crouching with eyes and muscles clenched.
Round and pebble smooth she effaces herself
under ripples of conversation and debate.
The woman in the block of ivory soap

has massive thighs that neigh,
great breasts that blare and strong arms that trumpet.
The woman of the golden fleece
laughs uproariously from the belly
inside the girl who imitates
a Christmas card virgin with glued hands,
who fishes for herself in other's eyes,
who stoops and creeps to make herself smaller.
In her bottled up is a woman peppery as curry,
a yam of a woman of butter and brass,
compounded of acid and sweet like a pineapple,
like a handgrenade set to explode,
like goldenrod ready to bloom.

Shameless Hussy (excerpt)
Alta

yesterday i had a wild thot. hearing james brown on the radio singing *say it loud: i'm black & i'm proud*. i thot, wonder how it would feel to say, say it loud, i'm female & proud. it was obviously too silly. think how embarrassed i would be if a neighbor came to the door. what if john came home & i was making the bed yelling I'M FEMALE & I'M PROUD? i'd never hear the end of it. i started saying it and nearly choked on the words. couldnt get them out. realized it was a lie. i aint proud. didnt have a thing to do with it. took pot luck and came out a broad. kept trying to say it. after a few tries, i could. it wasnt very loud. it was probly the quietest sound in the room. me patting pillows into place on the bed and muttering, *i'm female & i'm proud*. then i got a little hostile and said it loud, i'm female and proud and thot about it and wanted to feel it and said it loud i'm female and proud and after the record was over i yelled it a couple of times and it felt okay, and i havent done it since but maybe i will again.

Woman and Nature (excerpt)
Susan Griffin

The old woman who was wicked in her honesty asked questions of her mirror. When she was small she asked, "Why am I afraid of the dark? Why do I feel I will be devoured?" And her mirror answered, "Because you have reason to fear. You are small and you might be devoured. Because you are nothing but a shadow, a wisp, a seed, and you might be lost in the dark." And so she became large. Too large for devouring. From that tiny seed of a self a mighty form grew and now it was she who cast shadows. But after a while she came to the mirror again and asked, "Why am I afraid of my bigness?" And the mirror answered, "Because you are big. There is no disputing who you are. And it is not easy for you to hide." And so she began to stop hiding. She announced her presence. She even took joy in it. But still, when she looked in her mirror she saw herself and was frightened, and she asked the mirror why. "Because," the mirror said, "no one else sees what you see, no one else can tell you if what you see is true." So after that she decided to believe her own eyes. Once when she felt herself growing older, she said to the mirror, "Why am I afraid of birthdays?" "Because," the mirror said, "there is something you have always wanted to do which you have been afraid of doing and you know time is running out." And she ran from the mirror as quickly as she could because she knew in that moment she was not afraid and she wanted to seize the time. Over time, she and her mirror became friends, and the mirror would weep for her in compassion when her fears were real. Finally, her reflection asked her, "What do you still fear?" And the old woman answered, "I still fear death. I still fear change." And her mirror agreed. "Yes, they are frightening. Death is a closed door," the mirror flourished, "and change is a door hanging open."

"Yes, but fear is a key," laughed the wicked old woman, "and we still have our fears." She smiled.

Variation on a Theme by Rilke
(The Book of Hours, Book I, Poem 1, Stanza 1)
Denise Levertov

A certain day became a presence to me;
there it was, confronting me—a sky, air, light:
a being. And before it started to descend
from the height of noon, it leaned over
and struck my shoulder as if with

the flat of a sword, granting me
honor and a task. The day's blow
rang out, metallic—or it was I, a bell awakened,
and what I heard was my whole self
saying and singing what it knew: *I can.*

Stepping Westward
Denise Levertov

What is green in me
darkens, muscadine.

If woman is inconstant,
good, I am faithful to

ebb and flow, I fall
in season and now

is a time of ripening.
If her part

is to be true,
a north star,

good, I hold steady
in the black sky

and vanish by day,
yet burn there

in blue or above
quilts of cloud.

There is no savor
more sweet, more salt

than to be glad to be
what, woman,

and who, myself,
I am, a shadow

The Poem as Mask
Orpheus
Muriel Rukeyser

When I wrote of the women in their dances and wildness,
    it was a mask,
on their mountain, god-hunting, singing, in orgy,
it was a mask; when I wrote of the god,
fragmented, exiled from himself, his life, the love gone
    down with song,
it was myself, split open, unable to speak, in exile from
    myself.

There is no mountain, there is no god, there is memory
of my torn life, myself split open in sleep, the rescued child
beside me among the doctors, and a word
of rescue from the great eyes.

No more masks! No more mythologies!

Now, for the first time, the god lifts his hand,
the fragments join in me with their own music.

Outrage
Lucille Iverson

It is not so much
Cooking
But being cooked
That gets me;
When the chicken goes
In the oven
I'll be caught there too—
My head in the
Oven along with the
Gizzards and lungs—
One wing caught
With mine—
Heart, liver, entrails

Embroiled,
Boiled to a pink
Tasty succulence and then
Devoured.

Impaled on your
Incubi   I
Will not be nor
Stay to argue why
Not.   I
Who abandoned all
Who professed to love me—
Mother, father, brothers, aunts
     uncles, cousins, husband, child—
Know what love means:
Love
Is that which detains;
That magic of detention which you
Need from me,
But which tears a
Woman.

The power of Life is the
Integration of Life is the
Integration of Energy and
If you disintegrate,   I
Will not help you;
If you spatter
Red and bitter and
Rotten on the sidewalk,   I
Will not pick you up
Nor suckle you nor
Bathe your wounds nor
Mend your torn socks;—   I
A year ago would have said:
"Nestle your little broken head
On your mammy's breast,
You poor, broken
Child of the Universe;"
But now I say
Scram;   —I
May glance your way to
Laugh, and I
May toss you a penny;
For you, who have

Condemned me as
Witch, as
Mother,   —I
Have no more
Any pity;
For you who have
Despised me as
Succubi, as
Ball-breaker   —I
Tell you, you puke in
Your own folly.

My Passion is
Mine, nor am I
Vampire, nor
Banshee, nor
Screamer, nor
Waiting;   —I
Have turned away, and   I
Face a distance I
Have not run;   —I
Raise my fist beside the
Door of My Dreams and I
Take Time,
My Time,
All of it
In my Hands.

Woman in the Nineteenth Century (excerpt)
Margaret Fuller

I have urged on Woman independence of Man, not that I do not think the
sexes mutually needed by one another, but because in Woman this fact has led
to an excessive devotion, which has cooled love, degraded marriage, and pre-
vented either sex from being what it should be to itself or the other.

I wish Woman to live, *first* for God's sake. Then she will not make an
imperfect man her god, and thus sink to idolatry. Then she will not take what
is not fit for her from a sense of weakness and poverty. Then, if she finds what
she needs in Man embodied, she will know how to love, and be worthy of
being loved.

Offspring
Naomi Long Madgett

I tried to tell her:
    This way the twig is bent.
    Born of my trunk and strengthened by my roots,
    You must stretch newgrown branches
    Closer to the sun
    Than I can reach.
I wanted to say:
    Extend my self to that far atmosphere
    Only my dreams allow.

But the twig broke,
And yesterday I saw her
Walking down an unfamiliar street,
    Feet confident,
    Face slanted upward toward a threatening sky,
And
    She was smiling
    And she was
    Her very free,
    Her very individual,
    Unpliable
    Own.

Now I Become Myself
May Sarton

Now I become myself. It's taken
Time, many years and places;
I have been dissolved and shaken,
Worn other people's faces,
Run madly, as if Time were there,
Terribly old, crying a warning,
"Hurry, you will be dead before—"
(What? Before you reach the morning?
Or the end of the poem is clear?
Or love safe in the walled city?)
Now to stand still, to be here,

Feel my own weight and density!
The black shadow on the paper
Is my hand; the shadow of a word
As thought shapes the shaper
Falls heavy on the page, is heard.
All fuses now, falls into place
From wish to action, word to silence,
My work, my love, my time, my face
Gathered into one intense
Gesture of growing like a plant.
As slowly as the ripening fruit
Fertile, detached, and always spent,
Falls but does not exhaust the root,
So all the poem is, can give,
Grows in me to become the song,
Made so and rooted so by love.
Now there is time and Time is young.
O, in this single hour I live
All of myself and do not move.
I, the pursued, who madly ran,
Stand still, stand still, and stop the sun!

i am running into a new year
Lucille Clifton

i am running into a new year
and the old years blow back
like a wind
that i catch in my hair
like strong fingers like
all my old promises and
it will be hard to let go
of what i said to myself
about myself
when i was sixteen and
twentysix and thirtysix
even thirtysix but
i am running into a new year
and i beg what i love and
i leave to forgive me

Listen
Linda Lancione Moyer

Standing in the garden,
left hand laden
with ripe strawberries. The sun

beams off the glassy
backs of flies. Three
birds in the birch tree.

They must have been there
all year.

My mother, my grandmother,
stood like this
in their gardens,

I am 43.
This year I have planted my feet
on this ground

and am practicing
growing up out of my legs
like a tree.

Lilith and the Doctor
Kathleen Norris

He shuffled my file,
my life. I had lost the language of
trees in wind,
the river talking to stones.

He wrote in his notebooks:
how a chasm opened
in the ground at my feet;
how I almost drowned
in a whirlpool
that was just a bowl of dough.

And on a sunny afternoon
I'll never forget
the flowers seemed so brittle with cold
I knew they'd break
if I breathed on them.

"You're not constipated?" he asked.
"Do you have trouble getting to sleep?"
"No," I said, "I want to sleep all the time."
"Well, you don't have the clinical signs of depression," he said,
clicking his pen.

I left then, for good,
and as I walked
the song broke through,
the loud green sound
of this garden called the earth,
the garden between my thighs.
The sky's spinning song
of light and dark:
a rocking in my blood,
the ocean's lowing like a cow
looking for her calf.

I sat and sang by the water's edge
where I knew he would not go.

The Journey
Mary Oliver

One day you finally knew
what you had to do, and began,
though the voices around you
kept shouting
their bad advice—
though the whole house
began to tremble
and you felt the old tug
at your ankles.
"Mend my life!"
each voice cried.

But you didn't stop.
You knew what you had to do,
though the wind pried
with its stiff fingers
at the very foundations—
though their melancholy
was terrible.
It was already late
enough, and a wild night,
and the road full of fallen
branches and stones.
But little by little,
as you left their voices behind,
the stars began to burn
through the sheets of clouds,
and there was a new voice,
which you slowly
recognized as your own,
that kept you company
as you strode deeper and deeper
into the world,
determined to do
the only thing you could do—
determined to save
the only life you could save.

The Irises

Jeanne Foster

This afternoon I have taken the irises,
the yellow irises on long stems, from their livelihood.
I have cut them, one by one,
with somebody's leftover "Five and Ten Cent"
scissors, mine for these last seven years
of tenuous profession. I have taken them
irrespective of consideration
for others, who might feel some sense of
possession, living likewise in this sickly green
apartment building, others who might also need
to feast their eyes. I have taken them from
the patch overgrown with sage, now in purple blossom;
and golden California poppies, with a red

tulip stranded in the middle;
and a columbine, buried
among strawberries that have run rampant
in a year's time, barely turning
and eaten on the ground side by those fellows,
the slugs, who leave behind their saliva
and not themselves; and honeysuckle,
climbing the falling stucco.
I have taken the yellow irises up the fire stairs
in the back, up three flights,
to the rooms where I live,
for sunshine or hope or simple
stillness of heart or for self
appreciation. I have placed them
in a plain carafe on the white formica kitchen table,
because I have wanted to make love all day
and night enfolds me in strangely comfortable
covers, each of my limbs in its own caressing
tunnel of sheet, my head against the bosom of my pillow.
All these things speak their care for me.
And I have moved from sunlight,
lavishly expending itself on the backs
of buildings, into walls that hold me
for all they're worth, doing
everything they can to keep me safe,
holding me and my flowers, my selfish gift
of flowers, my sun, my light,
my yearning, the echoing halls
of my past, *nobody nobody nobody,*
the world slides west,
these yellow irises
are the opening.

Blue Morning Glory
Anne Pitkin

Voracious, yes. But when you see it,
shy blue flowers blaring like trumpets in spite of themselves,
centers star shaped and yellow; when it startles you,
early in the morning, all over a white picket fence, say,
in Massachusetts, you might think "triumphal," "prodigal,"
      "awake."

Of course you don't want it in your rose garden
among all the pruned, the decorous bushes. You don't want it
in the vegetables, for it will romp through the tomatoes,
beans and peas, will leave no room on the ground, or even
in the air, for the leafy lettuces and cabbages soberly
queueing up in their furrows. It will hog all the sky it can get,
knowing as it does what enormous thirst is satisfied by blue.

Father Michael says Follow the God of abundance.
Says we hurry from the moment's wealth
for fear it will be taken. Think of this:

the morning glory has been blossoming for so long
without permission that in some gardens it is no longer censored.
What does that tell you? See how it opens its tender throats
to a world that can sting it, how, without apology for its excess,
it blooms and blooms, though even yet
it seems surprised.

Housing Shortage
Naomi Replansky

I tried to live small.
I took a narrow bed.
I held my elbows to my sides.
I tried to step carefully
And to think softly
And to breathe shallowly
In my portion of air
And to disturb no one.

Yet see how I spread out and I cannot help it.
I take to myself more and more, and I take nothing
That I do not need, but my needs grow like weeds,
All over and invading; I clutter this place
With all the apparatus of living.
You stumble over it daily.

And then my lungs take their fill.
And then you gasp for air.

Excuse me for living,
But, since I am living,
Given inches, I take yards,
Taking yards, dream of miles,
And a landscape, unbounded
And vast in abandon.

You too dreaming the same.

Aging
(balm for a 27th birthday)
Erica Jong

Hooked for two years now on wrinkle creams   creams
    for
crowsfeet   ugly lines (if only there were one!)
any perfumed grease   which promises   youth   beauty
not truth   but all I need on earth
        I've been studying   how women age

                                how

it starts around the eyes   so you can tell
a woman of 22 from one of 28 merely by
a faint scribbling near the lids   a subtle crinkle
        a fine line
extending from the fields of vision

                                this

in itself is not unbeautiful   promising
        as it often does
insights which clear-eyed 22 has no inkling of
promising   certain sure-thighed things in bed
certain fingers on your spine & lids

                               but

it's only the beginning   as ruin proceeds downward
lingering for a while around the mouth   hardening the
    smile

into prearranged patterns (irreversible!)   writing fur-
         rows
from the wings of the nose   (oh nothing much at first
             but "showing promise"   like your early poems

                                                  of deepening)

& plotting lower to the corners of the mouth   droop-
         ing them
a little   like the tragic mask   though not at all gro-
         tesque
as yet   & then as you sidestep   into the 4th decade
beginning to crease the neck   (just slightly)
             though the breasts below

                                                  especially

when they're small (like mine) may stay high far
             into the thirties
still the neck will give you away   & after that the chin
which   though you may snip it back and hike it up
         under
your earlobes will never quite love your bones as it once
         did

                                                  though

the belly may be kept firm through numerous preg-
         nancies
by means of sit-ups   jogging   dancing   (think of Rus-
         sian ballerinas)
             & the cunt
as far as I know is ageless   possibly immortal   becom-
         ing simply
more open   more quick to understand   more dry-eyed
         than at 22

                                                  which

after all   is what you were dying for   (as you ravaged
islands of turtles   beehives   oysterbeds   the udders of
         cows)
desperate to censor changes which you simply might
         have let play

over you   lying back   listening   opening yourself
    letting the years make love the only way
    (poor blunderers)

                             they know

Advice

Ruth Stone

My hazard wouldn't be yours, not ever;
But every doom, like a hazelnut, comes down
To its own worm. So I am rocking here
Like any granny with her apron over her head
Saying, lordy me. It's my trouble.
There's nothing to be learned this way.
If I heard a girl crying help
I would go to save her;
But you hardly ever hear those words.
Dear children, you must try to say
Something when you are in need.
Don't confuse hunger with greed;
And don't wait until you are dead.

The Imperative of Intimacy

Women value human closeness. Though drawing near puts one at some risk, to be sure, it is in the touching of one with another that we become most fully ourselves. And the strong, sure presence of someone else warms the chill of the dark night. In the following selections, intimacy may exist between friends or between lovers or within the family, but at its best it includes a radical respect for the other and the willingness to be vulnerable.

Prayer for Revolutionary Love

Denise Levertov

That a woman not ask a man to leave meaningful work to
follow her.
That a man not ask a woman to leave meaningful work to
follow him.

That no one try to put Eros in bondage.
But that no one put a cudgel in the hands of Eros.

That our loyalty to one another and our loyalty to our work
not be set in false conflict.

That our love for each other give us love for each other's work.
That our love for each other's work give us love for one another.

That our love for each other's work give us love for one another.
That our love for each other give us love for each other's work.

That our love for each other, if need be,
give way to absence. And the unknown.

That we endure absence, if need be,
without losing our love for each other.
Without closing our doors to the unknown.

Out of My Time (excerpt)

Marya Mannes

. . . life demands that the duality in men and women be freed to function, released from hate or guilt. All wars derive from lack of empathy: the incapacity of one to understand and accept the likeness or difference of another. Whether in nations or the encounters of race and sex, competition then replaces compassion; subjection excludes mutuality.

Only through this duality in each can a man and woman have empathy for each other. The best lovers are men who can imagine and even feel the specific pleasures of women; women who know the passions and vulnerabilities of the penis—triumphant or tender—in themselves.

Without empathy, men and women, husbands and wives, become tools of each other: competitors, rivals, master and slave, buyer and seller. In this war the aggressions of the wholly 'feminine' woman are just as destructive (mostly to the male) as the aggressions of the wholly 'masculine' man.

For centuries the need to prove this image of masculinity has lain at the root of death: the killing of self and others in the wars of competition and conquest; the perversion of humanity itself.

We need each other's qualities if we are ever to understand each other in love and life. The beautiful difference of our biological selves will not diminish through this mutual fusion. It should indeed flower, expand; blow the mind as well as the flesh. When women can cherish the vulnerability of men as much as men can exult in the strength of women, a new breed could lift a ruinous yoke from both. We could both breathe free.

Councils
Marge Piercy

We must sit down
and reason together.
We must sit down:
men standing want to hold forth.
They rain down upon faces lifted.
We must sit down on the floor
on the earth
on stones and mats and blankets.
There must be no front to the speaking
no platform, no rostrum,
no stage or table.
We will not crane
to see who is speaking.
Perhaps we should sit in the dark.
In the dark we could utter our feelings.
In the dark we could propose
and describe and suggest.
In the dark we could not see who speaks
and only the words
would say what they say.
No one would speak more than twice.
No one would speak less than once.
Thus saying what we feel and what we want,
what we fear for ourselves and each other

into the dark, perhaps we could begin
to begin to listen.
Perhaps we should talk in groups
the size of new families,
not more, never more than twenty.
Perhaps we should start by speaking softly.
The women must learn to dare to speak,
The men must learn to bother to listen.
The women must learn to say I think this is so.
The men must learn to stop dancing solos on the ceiling.
After each speaks, she or he
will say a ritual phrase:
It is not I who speaks but the wind.
Wind blows through me.
Long after me, is the wind.

To have without holding

Marge Piercy

Learning to love differently is hard,
love with the hands wide open, love
with the doors banging on their hinges,
the cupboard unlocked, the wind
roaring and whimpering in the rooms
rustling the sheets and snapping the blinds
that thwack like rubber bands
in an open palm.

It hurts to love wide open
stretching the muscles that feel
as if they are made of wet plaster,
then of blunt knives, then
of sharp knives.

It hurts to thwart the reflexes
of grab, of clutch; to love and let
go again and again. It pesters to remember
the lover who is not in the bed,
to hold back what is owed to the work
that gutters like a candle in a cave
without air, to love consciously,
conscientiously, concretely, constructively.

I can't do it, you say it's killing
me, but you thrive, you glow
on the street like a neon raspberry,
You float and sail, a helium balloon
bright bachelor's button blue and bobbing
on the cold and hot winds of our breath,
as we make and unmake in passionate
diastole and systole the rhythm
of our unbound bonding, to have
and not to hold, to love
with minimized malice, hunger
and anger moment by moment balanced.

Paris and Helen
Judy Grahn

He called her: golden dawn
She called him: the wind whistles

He called her: heart of the sky
She called him: message bringer

He called her: mother of pearl,
    barley woman, rice provider,
    millet basket, corn maid,
    flax princess, all-maker, weef

She called him: fawn, roebuck,
    stag, courage, thunderman,
    all-in-green, mountain strider,
    keeper of forests, my-love-rides

He called her: the tree is
She called him: bird dancing

He called her: who stands,
    has stood, will always stand
She called him: arriver

He called her: the heart and the womb
    are similar
She called him: arrow in my heart.

Pornography and Silence (excerpt)
Susan Griffin

To make love is to become like this infant again. We grope with our mouths toward the body of another being, whom we trust, who takes us in her arms. We rock together with this loved one. We move beyond speech. Our bodies move past all the controls we have learned. We cry out in ecstasy, in feeling. We are back in a natural world before culture tried to erase our experience of nature. In this world, to touch another is to express love; there is no idea apart from feeling, and no feeling which does not ring through our bodies and our souls at once.

This is eros. Our own wholeness. Not the sensation of pleasure alone, nor the idea of love alone, but the whole experience of human love.

Growing Together
Joyce Carol Oates

we have tangled together
too often
our sleep has tangled mossy and sinister
as old rocks
our faces pressed together in sleep
have taken on the slumber of rocks, rocks' faces,
which are the least important part
of rocks

the veins of your forehead have swollen
like vines
my hair has grown too long
down onto your chest
our toenails outlined in harmless old dirt
scrape against all our legs
for weeks

we have embraced
too often
our arms have tangled slick with sweat
like the sweat of oil on water
making phosphorescent
the swimmers and their innocent limbs

the glow shows them everywhere
no escape in any dark

rising, pulling back my long sweaty hair
I see a face in the mirror only half mine
what I am thinking is only half mine
these words are only half mine
the frayed threads of our bodies want
only that tangling again
that old growing together again
a completion like the exhaling
of a single breath

After Love
Maxine Kumin

Afterwards, the compromise.
Bodies resume their boundaries.

These legs, for instance, mine.
Your arms take you back in.

Spoons of our fingers, lips
admit their ownership.

The bedding yawns, a door
blows aimlessly ajar

and overhead, a plane
singsongs coming down.

Nothing is changed, except
there was a moment when

the wolf, the mongering wolf
who stands outside the self

lay lightly down, and slept.

A Thought

Linda Hogan

The tree is all alone.
Its fruit is swollen with rain.
Yes, it is haggard,
the branches are bent down
and the leaves have gone dark.
The rain has added still another burden
and the red birds are too heavy in it.
They sing from the branches
and yes it is kneeling even more
and the birds are eating the black cherries.
When they leave,
the branches rise up after them.

So you came to surprise me
while I was watching the lonely tree
and red birds. So you are here
putting a thought in my mind.
Let's kneel down
through all the worlds of the body
like lovers. I know
I am a tree and full of life
and I know you, you
are the flying one and will leave.
But can't we swallow the sweetness
and can't you sing in my arms
and sleep in the human light
of the sun and moon I have been
drinking alone.
Later we will rise up
and shake the sleep from our arms
and find we were not broken down
at all.

New Mother
Sharon Olds

A week after our child was born,
you cornered me in the spare room
and we sank down on the bed.
You kissed me and kissed me, my milk undid its
burning slip-knot through my nipples,
soaking my shirt. All week I had smelled of milk,
fresh milk, sour. I began to throb:
my sex had been torn easily as cloth by the
crown of her head, I'd been cut with a knife and
sewn, the stitches pulling at my skin—
and the first time you're broken, you don't know
you'll be healed again, better than before.
I lay in fear and blood and milk
while you kissed and kissed me, your lips hot and swollen
as a teen-age boy's, your sex dry and big,
all of you so tender, you hung over me,
over the nest of the stitches, over the
splitting and tearing, with the patience of someone who
finds a wounded animal in the woods
and stays with it, not leaving its side
until it is whole, until it can run again.

Dancing the Shout to the True Gospel or
The Song Movement Sisters
Don't Want Me to Sing
Rita Mae Brown

I follow the scent of a woman
Melon heavy
Ripe with joy
Inspiring me
To rip great holes in the night
So the sun blasts through
And this is all I shall ever know
Her breath
Filling the hollows of my neck
A luxury diminishing death.

Late Autumn
May Sarton

On random wires the rows of summer swallows
Wait for their lift-off. They will soon be gone
Before All Saints and before All Hallows,
The changing time when we are most alone.

Disarmed, too vulnerable, full of dread,
And once again as naked as the trees
Before the dark, precarious days ahead
And troubled skies over tumultuous seas.

When we are so transparent to the dead
There is no wall. We hear their voices speak,
And as the small birds wheel off overhead
We bend toward the earth suddenly weak.

How to believe that all will not be lost?
Our flowers, too, not perish in the blight?
Love, leave me your South against the frost.
Say "hush" to my fears, and warm the night.

The Way Towards Each Other
Jeni Couzyn

The way towards each other is through our bodies.
Words are the longest distance you can travel
so complex and hazardous you
lose your direction.

Time is no way either. A river mouth it opens
to a mixing of waters, a tidal
diffusion, never
a consummation.

In our bodies we are fallen in a thorn thicket.
Out is a tearing apart, a letting of juices
Inside though is a pathway, a tremulous compensation—
the possibility of touching.

Blossom

Mary Oliver

In April
    the ponds
        open
            like black blossoms,
the moon
    swims in every one;
        there's fire
            everywhere: frogs shouting
their desire,
    their satisfaction. What
        we know: that time
            chops at us all like an iron
hoe, that death
    is a state of paralysis. What
        we long for: joy
            before death, nights
in the swale—everything else
    can wait but not
        this thrust
            from the root
of the body. What
    we know: we are more
        than blood—we are more
            than our hunger and yet
we belong
    to the moon and when the ponds
        open, when the burning
            begins the most
thoughtful among us dreams
    of hurrying down
        into the black petals,
        into the fire,
into the night where time lies shattered,
into the body of another.

To Drink

Jane Hirshfield

I want to gather your darkness
in my hands, to cup it like water
and drink.
I want this in the same way
as I want to touch your cheek—
it is the same—
the way a moth will come
to the bedroom window in late September,
beating and beating its wings against cold glass;
the way a horse will lower
his long head to water, and drink,
and pause to lift his head and look,
and drink again,
taking everything in with the water,
everything.

Medicine

Alice Walker

Grandma sleeps with
my sick
    grand-
pa so she
can get him
during the night
medicine
to stop
  the pain

   In
the morning
  clumsily
   I
wake
  them

Her eyes
look at me
from under-
               neath
his withered
arm

  The
medicine
  is all
    in
her long
  un-
        braided
               hair.

Love Is Not Concerned
Alice Walker

love is not concerned
with whom you pray
or where you slept
the night you ran away
from home
love is concerned
that the beating of your heart
should kill no one.

The Hug
Tess Gallagher

A woman is reading a poem on the street
and another woman stops to listen. We stop too,
with our arms around each other. The poem
is being read and listened to out here
in the open. Behind us
no one is entering or leaving the houses.

Suddenly a hug comes over me and I'm
giving it to you, like a variable star shooting light
off to make itself comfortable, then
subsiding. I finish but keep on holding
you. A man walks up to us and we know he hasn't
come out of nowhere, but if he could, he
would have. He looks homeless because of how
he needs. "Can I have one of those?" he asks you,
and I feel you nod. I'm surprised,
surprised you don't tell him how
it is—that I'm yours, only
yours, etc., exclusive as a nose to
its face. Love—that's what we're talking about, love
that nabs you with "for me
only" and holds on.

So I walk over to him and put my
arms around him and try to
hug him like I mean it. He's got an overcoat on
so thick I can't feel
him past it. I'm starting the hug
and thinking, "How big a hug is this supposed to be?
How long shall I hold this hug?" Already
we could be eternal, his arms falling over my
shoulders, my hands not
meeting behind his back, he is so big!

I put my head into his chest and snuggle
in. I lean into him. I lean my blood and my wishes
into him. He stands for it. This is his
and he's starting to give it back so well I know he's
getting it. This hug. So truly, so tenderly
we stop having arms and I don't know if
my lover has walked away or what, or
if the woman is still reading the poem, or the houses—
what about them?—the houses.

Clearly, a little permission is a dangerous thing.
But when you hug someone you want it
to be a masterpiece of connection, the way the button
on his coat will leave the imprint of
a planet in my cheek
when I walk away. When I try to find some place
to go back to.

Nikki-Rosa
Nikki Giovanni

childhood remembrances are always a drag
if you're Black
you always remember things like living in Woodlawn
with no inside toilet
and if you become famous or something
they never talk about how happy you were to have
your mother
all to yourself and
how good the water felt when you got your bath
from one of those
big tubs that folk in chicago barbecue in
and somehow when you talk about home
it never gets across how much you
understood their feelings
as the whole family attended meetings about Hollydale
and even though you remember
your biographers never understand
your father's pain as he sells his stock
and another dream goes
And though you're poor it isn't poverty that
concerns you
and though they fought a lot
it isn't your father's drinking that makes any difference
but only that everybody is together and you
and your sister have happy birthdays and very good
Christmasses
and I really hope no white person ever has cause
to write about me
because they never understand
Black love is Black wealth and they'll
probably talk about my hard childhood
and never understand that
all the while I was quite happy

Feast Day (excerpt)
Ellen Bryant Voigt

                                O mild Christ,
the long plank table is spread with wealth
and everyone is gathered. The father puts aside
the quarrel with his one remaining son, the mother
wipes an eye on her apron, the daughters hush,
the cousins cease their cruel competition.
On the table, the brass centerpiece is heaped
with the brilliant red beads of pyracantha,
thorn of fire, torn from a low shrub beside the house;
and lifted above them—emblem of peace, emblem of affection—
the fleshy leaves of mistletoe, bearing its few pearls,
its small inedible berry.

Ironing Their Clothes
Julia Alvarez

With a hot glide up, then down, his shirts,
I ironed out my father's back, cramped
and worried with work. I stroked the yoke,
the breast pocket, collar and cuffs,
until the rumpled heap relaxed into the shape
of my father's broad chest, the shoulders shrugged off
the world, the collapsed arms spread for a hug.
And if there'd been a face above the buttondown neck,
I would have pressed the forehead out, I would
have made a boy again out of that tired man!

If I clung to her skirt as she sorted the wash
or put out a line, my mother frowned,
a crease down each side of her mouth.
This is no time for love! But here
I could linger over her wrinkled bedjacket,
kiss at the damp puckers of her wrists
with the hot tip. Here I caressed complications
of darts, scallops, ties, pleats which made
her outfits test of the patience of my passion.
Here I could lay my dreaming iron on her lap. . . .

The smell of baked cotton rose from the board
and blew with a breeze out the window
to the family wardrobe drying on the clothesline,
all needing a touch of my iron. Here I could tickle
the underarms of my big sister's petticoat
or secretly pat the backside of her pajamas.
For she too would have warned me not to muss
her fresh blouses, starched jumpers, and smocks,
all that my careful hand had ironed out,
forced to express my excess love on cloth.

7 : 3 *(excerpt)*
Alta

love is believable.
keep that as a smooth stone, for sometimes you will be the
only one to love. for sometimes, you will be hated, & all the
love within reach will have to be your own, & what you can
tap from the spirits who fly to be with us at those moments,
& lend us their wings. who land on the lamps to give us comfort & courage, when we think we have nothing to say. when
we have nothing to say, perhaps it is time to listen.
                          to take dictation from the saints of
the past, without judgement can one say that, "saints," without judgement, can one love, can one seek out people who
make one feel good. without judgement, can one survive, buying food. without judgement. casting our pearls.

love is free, sometimes, & costly othertimes. we may only
have each other. our true touch. we may only have.

2 : 7 *(excerpt)*
Alta

loving your neighbor is all very fine when you have nice
neighbors. this is why people choose the town they live in.
we all want nice neighbors. it's the folks in the *next* town
who are the bad guys. you'd be amazed at how citified folks

hate the people in the suburbs. not the suburbs, the people
in them. but would they want us living next door? i ask you.

& joan of arc was noisy. she must have made a lousy neighbor. & jesus, giving everything away - & ghandi, a walking
guilt trip. some people make nicer neighbors than others.
but there you have it. city planning.

funny how essays on politics, on war & peace, seem to talk
about love.

The Big Heart
Anne Sexton

"Too many things are occurring for even a big heart to hold."
—From an essay by W. B. Yeats

Big heart,
wide as a watermelon,
but wise as birth,
there is so much abundance
in the people I have:
Max, Lois, Joe, Louise,
Joan, Marie, Dawn,
Arlene, Father Dunne,
and all in their short lives
give to me repeatedly,
in the way the sea
places its many fingers on the shore,
again and again
and they know me,
they help me unravel,
they listen with ears made of conch shells,
they speak back with the wine of the best region.
They are my staff.
They comfort me.

They hear how
the artery of my soul has been severed
and soul is spurting out upon them,
bleeding on them,

messing up their clothes,
dirtying their shoes.
And God is filling me,
though there are times of doubt
as hollow as the Grand Canyon,
still God is filling me.
He is giving me the thoughts of dogs,
the spider in its intricate web,
the sun
in all its amazement,
and a slain ram
that is the glory,
the mystery of great cost,
and my heart,
which is very big,
I promise it is very large,
a monster of sorts,
takes it all in—
all in comes the fury of love.

Centering (excerpt)
Mary Caroline Richards

But how are we to love when we are stiff and numb and disinterested? How are we to transform ourselves into limber and soft organisms lying open to the world at the quick? By what process and what agency do we perform the Great Work, transforming lowly materials into gold? Love, like its counterpart Death, is a yielding at the center. Not in the sentiment. Nor in the genitals. Look deep into my eyes and see the love-light. Figured forth in intelligent cooperation, sensitive congeniality, physical warmth. At the center the love must live.

One gives up all one has for this. This is the love that resides in the self, the self-love, out of which all love pours. The fountain, the source. At the center. One gives up all the treasured sorrow and self-mistrust, all the precious loathing and suspicion, all the secret triumphs of withdrawal. One bends in the wind. There are many disciplines that strengthen one's athleticism for love. It takes all one's strength. And yet it takes all one's weakness too. Sometimes it is only by having all one's so-called strength pulverized that one is weak enough, strong enough, to yield. It takes that power of nature in one which is neither strength nor weakness but closer perhaps to *virtu*, person, personalized energy. Do not speak about strength and weakness, manliness and womanliness, aggressive-ness and submissiveness. Look at this flower. Look at this child. Look at this rock with lichen growing on it. Listen to this gull scream as he drops through the air to gobble the bread I throw and clumsily rights himself in the wind. Bear ye one another's burdens, the Lord said, and he was talking law.

Love is not a doctrine, Peace is not an international agreement. Love and Peace are beings who live as possibilities in us.

Mothering

The following section contains poems about pregnancy and birth as well as selections about motherhood. The experiences of carrying a child and of birthing are presented as sacred: bringing forth life is the holiest of the holy. Several poems express the mixed blessings of parenthood; others treat the special relationship between mother and daughter.

Advent

Kathleen Norris

They are fruit
and transport:
ripening melons,
prairie schooners journeying
under full sail.

Susan worries that her water will break
on the subway. New York is full of grandmothers;
someone will take care of her.
Kate has been ordered to bed.
A Wyoming wind like wild horses
brushes snow against her window.
Charlotte feels like a ripe papaya.
"The body's such a humble thing," she says,
afloat in her kitchen
in Honolulu,
unable to see her feet.

Pregnant women stand like sentinels,
they protect me
while I sleep. They part the sea
and pass down the bloody length of it,
until we are strangers
ready to be born,
strangers who will suffer and die.

They are home
and exile, beginning and end,
end and means.
I am more ordinary. Still, I listen
as the holy wind breathes through them.
I make a little song
in praise of bringing forth.

Early Morning Woman
Joy Harjo

early morning woman
rising   the sun
    the woman
bending and stretching
with the strength of the child
that moves
in her belly

early morning makes her
a woman that she is
the sun
is her beginning
it is the strength
that guides her child

early morning woman
she begins that way
    the sun
    the child
are the moving circle
beginning with the woman
in the early morning

Poems for the New
Kathleen Fraser

  1
we're connecting,
   foot under my rib.
I'm sore with life!
At night,
   your toes grow. Inches of the new!
The lion prowls the sky
and shakes his tail for you.
Pieces of moon
   fly by my kitchen window.

And your father comes
riding the lion's back
        in the dark,
to hold me,
      you,
        in the perfect circle of him.

2
Voluptuous against him, I am
nothing superfluous,
but all—
bones, bark of him, root of him take.
I am round
with his sprouting,
new thing new thing!
He wraps me.
The sheets are white.
My belly has tracks on it—
        hands and feet
are moving
under this taut skin.
In snow, in light,
we are about to become!

Magnificat
Chana Bloch

1
Now the fingers and toes are formed,
the doctor says.
Nothing to worry about. Nothing
to worry about

2
I will carry my belly to the mountain!
I will bare it to the moon, let the wolves howl,
I will wear it forever.
I will hold it up every morning in my ten fingers,
crowing
to wake the world.

3

This flutter that comes with me everywhere
is it my fear

or is it your jointed fingers
is it your feet

4

You are growing yourself
out   of   nothing:
there's   nothing
at last   I   can
do: I   stop
doing: you
are

5

Miles off in the dark,
my dark,
you head for dry land,

naked, safe
in salt waters.

Tides lap you.

Your breathing
makes me an ark.

The Wife Takes a Child
Ellen Bryant Voigt

She has come next door to practice our piano.
Fat worms, her fingers hover over the keys,
dolce, dolce, advance to a black note.
I call out answers: she blinks a trusting eye.
From the window I can see the phlox
bank and flower, the violets' broad train
at the yard's edge, and beyond, the bee-boxes,
each one baited for summer with a queen.

Love, how long must we reproduce ourselves
in the neighbors' children, bees in false hives,
bright inviting blossoms, mine for a season.
Against the C-scale's awkward lullabye
I carry the offense of my flat belly,
the silent red loss of monthly bleeding.

Birth
George Ella Lyon

In the steel room
where one becomes two
we were delivered.
But for a moment
I saw the rope
blue, shiny between us;
then it was cut
tied without pain
being heartbeat and no nerve.

As you wailed in your heated bed
a nurse held the pan so I could see
that valentine we all arrive with,
that red pad of which you were the lily
with the cord lying bleached across it
like a root pulled from the water
like a heartroot torn free.

Rising to Meet It
Chana Bloch

Today I woke up missing
the pain of childbirth. The pain, not
the fixed clock-stare of the walls
or the fingers
combing my tangled hair.

All that night I lay
tethered to my breathing.
Ride out the waves, the doctor said.

The first time I touched a man,
what startled me more than the pleasure
was knowing what to do.
I turned to him with
a motion so firm it must have been
forming inside me
before I was born.

Pain is the salty element. Strapped
to the long night,
I struck out for land, sure strokes, the body
solid, bucking for breath, slippery,
wet. An ocean
rolled off my shoulders.

Today I woke up groping, and missed
the simple
pain of childbirth—
                              No, not the pain
but that rising to meet it like a body
rising toward pleasure,
buoyant, athletic, sure of its power.

Now That I Am Forever with Child
Audre Lorde

How the days went
while you were blooming within me
I remember each upon each—
the swelling changed planes of my body
and how you first fluttered, then jumped
and I thought it was my heart.

How the days wound down
and the turning of winter
I recall, with you growing heavy
against the wind. I thought

now her hands
are formed, and her hair
has started to curl
now her teeth are done
now she sneezes.
Then the seed opened
I bore you one morning just before spring
My head rang like a fiery piston
my legs were towers between which
A new world was passing.

Since then
I can only distinguish
one thread within running hours
You, flowing through selves
toward You.

The Network of the Imaginary Mother (excerpt)
Robin Morgan

Little heart, little heart,
you have sung in me like the spiral alder-bud.
You, who gave birth to this mother
comprehend—for how much longer?—my mysteries.
Son of my cellular reincarnation, you alone know
the words that awaken me when I play dead
in our game. You alone wave
at the wisp through which I see you.
You understand. You whisper,
"Listen—life is really going on, right now,
around us. Do you see it? Sometimes I lose it
but if I sit still and listen, it comes back,
and then I think, How funny, this is what being alive is.
Do you know?"
I have uttered you wisely.

Still, I have grieved before the time, in preparation
for my dolor, at how you will become
a grown male child, tempted by false gods.
I have been *Pisaura mirabilis*, the nursery-web spider

who carries her egg's bulk in aching jaws,
who wraps it in a weft of love,
who guards its hatching.
You have clung to me like a spiderling
to the back of the *Lycosa lenta,* Wolf-spider mother,
I have waited, whenever you fell off,
for you to scramble on again before proceeding.
But you have come five-fold years
and what I know now is nothing
can abduct you fully from the land where you were born.

*

Wars have been made against me, empires built
with the dolmen of my bones, ships have pocked
the egg of my covenant where it gleams
on their benighted path.
But there is no erasing this:
the central memory of what we are
to one another, the grove of ritual.
I have set my seal upon you.

I say:
you shall be a child of the mother
as of old, and your face will not be turned from me.

The Network of the Imaginary Mother (excerpt)
Robin Morgan

And this is the fragrance, almost forgotten,
that warms the deepest dreams of us all—
even the large male children who grow
to fear, or conquer, or imitate its power;
even the large female children who find ourselves
rocking each other, or men, or babies—
we, the living totems of that rhythmic breast
that rocked us, and which we have become,
yet long for still.

*

Why have I called you "Mother" in my dreams?

Alta

sometimes I dont understand you. sometimes i sit helpless in
a chair while you scream. last year you started slugging me
when i spanked you. i didnt hit my mom back till i was 16.
you can climb every tree here. all the way past the roof
on the plum tree, up the limbless trunk of the walnut. we
forget you're 7 years old so when you cry cause your foot
hurts its like a surprise.
last nite you explained to the fussy baby, - everybody has to
go nite nite. lolo has to go nite nite, angel has to go nite nite.
mommy has to go nite nite. - -mommy? nite nite?- - yeah,
even mommy has to go nite nite. - i stand outside your door
cause your voice comforts me. when you were tiny & i would
tuck you in, you patted me even in your sleep.

Unspoken
Judith Ortiz Cofer

to my daughter

When I hug you tight at bedtime,
you wince in pain for the tender
swelling of new breasts.
Nothing is said, both of us aware
of the convenant of silence
we must maintain through the rending
apart that is adolescence.
                    But it won't always
be confusion and hurting, the body
will find itself through this pain;
remember Michelangelo, who believed
that in marble, form already exists,
the artist's hands simply pulling it out
into the world.
                    I want to tell you about men:
the pleasure of a lover's hands on skin
you think may rip at elbows and knees
stretching over a frame like clothes

you've almost outgrown; of the moment
when a woman first feels
a baby's mouth at her breast, opening her
like the hand of God in Genesis, the moment
when all that led to this seems right.
                    Instead I say, *sweet dreams,*
for the secrets hidden under the blanket
like a forbidden book
I'm not supposed to know you've read.

Happy Birthday
Alicia Ostriker

Happy birthday, a gray day like the first one—
You were so brave to enter our world
With its dirty rain, its look of a sepia photograph.

I call you at college, early and drowsy.
I hear you describe the party last night,
How you danced, how dancing is one of the things

You love in your life, like thinking hard. You are
All right, then, and on the telephone
Hearing the high snare drum of your voice

I can feel you about to be born, I can feel
The barriers yield as you slide
Along the corrugated glitter,

Like some terrible rubbery ocean built of blood
That parts at a touch, leaving a path.
What should I do, you wonder, *after I graduate?*

I imagine you curled under your quilt
As a cold light begins to come in where you are
Like a knife in a pirate's teeth. Dear salt flesh,

I am ready if you are, I am afraid if you are.
I still ask: will it hurt, will it give pleasure?
Of course it will. On your mark, get set,

We give birth to each other. Welcome. Welcome.

Mothers, Daughters
Shirley Kaufman

Through every night we hate,
preparing the next day's
war. She bangs the door.
Her face laps up my own
despair, the sour, brown eyes,
the heavy hair she won't
tie back. She's cruel,
as if my private meanness
found a way to punish us.
We gnaw at each other's
skulls. Give me what's mine.
I'd haul her back, choking
myself in her, herself
in me. There is a book
called *Poisons* on her shelf.
Her room stinks with incense,
animal turds, hamsters
she strokes like silk. They
exercise on the bathroom
floor, and two drop through
the furnace vent. The whole
house smells of the accident,
the hot skins, the small
flesh rotting. Six days
we turn the gas up then
to fry the dead. I'd fry
her head if I could until
she cried love, love me!

All she won't let me do.
Her stringy figure in
the windowed room shares
its thin bones with no one.
Only her shadow on the glass
waits like an older sister.
Now she stalks, leans forward,
concentrates merely on getting
from here to there. Her feet
are bare. I hear her breathe
where I can't get in. If I
break through to her, she will
drive nails into my tongue.

The Bad Mother

Susan Griffin

The bad mother wakes from dreams
of imperfection trying to be perfection.
All night she's engineered a train
too heavy with supplies
to the interior. She fails.
The child she loves
has taken on bad habits, cigarettes
maybe even drugs. She
recognizes lies. You don't
fool me, she wants to say,
the bad mother, ready to play
and win.
This lamb who's gone—
this infant she is
pinioned to—does not listen,
she drives with all her magic down a
different route to darkness where
all life begins.

Black Mother Woman
Audre Lorde

I cannot recall you gentle.
Through your heavy love
I have become
an image of your once delicate flesh
split with deceitful longings.
When strangers come and compliment me
your aged spirit takes a bow
jingling with pride
but once you hid that secret
in the center of furies
hanging me
with deep breasts and wiry hair
with your own split flesh and long suffering eyes
buried in myths of no worth.

But I have peeled away your anger
down to its core of love
and look mother
I am
a dark temple where your true spirit rises
beautiful and tough as a chestnut
stanchion against your nightmares of weakness
and if my eyes conceal
a squadron of conflicting rebellions
I learned from you
to define myself
through your denials.

February 13, 1980
Lucille Clifton

twenty-one years of my life you have been
the lost color in my eye. my secret blindness,
all my seeings turned grey with your going.
mother, i have worn your name like a shield.
it has torn but protected me all these years,

now even your absence comes of age.
i put on a dress called woman for this day
but i am not grown away from you
whatever i say.

One Writer's Beginnings (excerpt)
Eudora Welty

Even as we grew up, my mother could not help imposing herself between her children and whatever it was they might take it in mind to reach out for in the world. For she would get it for them, if it was good enough for them—she would have to be very sure—and give it to them, at whatever cost to herself: valiance was in her very fibre. She stood always prepared in herself to challenge the world in our place. She did indeed tend to make the world look dangerous, and so it had been to her. A way had to be found around her love sometimes, without challenging *that*, and at the same time cherishing it in its unassailable strength. Each of us children did, sooner or later, in part at least, solve this in a different, respectful, complicated way.

But I think she was relieved when I chose to be a writer of stories, for she thought writing was safe.

The Measure of My Days (excerpt)
Florida Scott-Maxwell

A mother's love for her children, even her inability to let them be, is because she is under a painful law that the life that passed through her must be brought to fruition. Even when she swallows it whole she is only acting like any frightened mother cat eating its young to keep it safe. It is not easy to give closeness and freedom, safety plus danger.

No matter how old a mother is she watches her middle-aged children for signs of improvement. It could not be otherwise for she is impelled to know that the seeds of value sown in her have been winnowed. She never outgrows the burden of love, and to the end she carries the weight of hope for those she bore. Oddly, very oddly, she is forever surprised and even faintly wronged that her sons and daughters are just people, for many mothers hope and half expect that their new-born child will make the world better, will somehow be a redeemer. Perhaps they are right, and they can believe that the rare quality they glimpsed in the child is active in the burdened adult.

Mother
Sharon Mayer Libera

Mother, I may do violence to you:
Extract a group of proverbs from your flow
Of talk, punctuate your letters, renew
Your beauty from yellow photos that show
You happy. Or, again, I may blacken
Your prejudices, even sour your breath,
Describe in detail what did not happen
But in nightmare: myself strangled to death
By the life-stalk. I do not mean to bruise
Your sweet breasts with hard words. Forgive the child
In me that to construct its world must use
Prime matter, and on its own wall sees wild
Shapes. But not tonight, when curled on your feet
You read and doze, too real for me, too deep.

Each Bird Walking
Tess Gallagher

Not while, but long after he had told me,
I thought of him, washing his mother, his
bending over the bed and taking back
the covers. There was a basin of water
and he dipped a washrag in and
out of the basin, the rag
dripping a little onto the sheet as he
turned from the bedside to the nightstand
and back, there being no place

on her body he shouldn't touch because
he had to and she helped him, moving
the little she could, lifting so he could
wipe under her arms, a dipping motion
in the hollow. Then working up from
the feet, around the ankles, over the
knees. And this last, opening
her thighs and running the rag firmly
and with the cleaning thought

up through her crotch, between the lips,
over the V of thin hairs—

as though he were a mother
who had the excuse of cleaning to touch
with love and indifference,
the secret parts of her child, to graze
the sleepy sexlessness in its waiting
to find out what to do for the sake
of the body, for the sake of what only
the body can do for itself.

So his hand, softly at the place
of his birth-light. And she, eyes deepened
and closed in the dim room.
And because he told me her death as
important to his being with her,
I could love him another way. Not
of the body alone, or of its making,
but carried in the white spires of trembling
until what spirit, what breath we were
was shaken from us. Small then,
the word *holy.*

He turned her on her stomach
and washed the blades of her shoulders, the
small of the back. "That's good," she said,
"that's enough."
On our lips that morning, the tart juice
of the mothers, so strong in remembrance, no
asking, no giving, and what you said, this
being the end of our loving, so as not to hurt
the closer one to you, made me look
to see what was left of us
with our sex taken away. "Tell me," I said,
"something I can't forget." Then the story of
your mother, and when you finished
I said, "That's good, that's enough."

35/10
Sharon Olds

Brushing out my daughter's dark
silken hair before the mirror
I see the grey gleaming on my head,
the silver-haired servant behind her. Why is it
just as we begin to go
they begin to arrive, the fold in my neck
clarifying as the fine bones of her
hips sharpen? As my skin shows
its dry pitting, she opens like a small
pale flower on the tip of a cactus;
as my last chances to bear a child
are falling through my body, the duds among them,
her full purse of eggs, round and
firm as hard-boiled yolks, is about
to snap its clasp. I brush her tangled
fragrant hair at bedtime. It's an old
story—the oldest we have on our planet—
the story of replacement.

Generations

Women seem especially sensitive to the cycles of life: there are those who have gone before and have prepared the way for present life; in turn, present life will give way to new. Thus it has been, and thus it will be forevermore. It is appropriate to give thanks. And it is for us to take the best of what we have been given and carry it forward into the future for our children and our children's children.

Dandelion Greens
Jane Flanders

You must come back, as your grandmother did,
with her basket and sharp knife, in daffodil light,
to the pasture, where the best greens spring
from heaps of dung, dark in the still brown
meadow grass. Cut them close to the root,
before they flower, rinse them in rain water
and bring them to the table, tossed
with oil, vinegar and salt, or homemade dressing.

They will be bitter but rich in iron—
your spring tonic, your antidote to sleep.
Eat them because they are good for you.
Eat them in joy, for the earth revives.
Eat them in remembrance of your grandmother,
who raised ten children on them. Think
of all the dandelions they picked for her,
the countless downy seeds their laughter spread.

This is the life we believe in—
the saw-toothed blades, the lavish, common flowers.

Keeping Hair
Ramona Wilson

My grandmother had braids
at the thickest, pencil wide
held with bright wool
cut from her bed shawl.
No teeth left but white hair
combed and wet carefully
early each morning.
The small wild plants found among stones
on the windy and brown plateaus
revealed their secrets to her hand
and yielded to her cooking pots.
She made a sweet amber water
from willows,

boiling the life out
to pour onto her old head.
"It will keep your hair."
She bathed my head once
rain water not sweeter.
The thought that once
when I was so very young
her work-bent hands
very gently and smoothly
washed my hair in willows
may also keep my heart.

Matmiya
Mary TallMountain

for my Grandmother

I see you sitting
Implanted by roots
Coiled deep from your thighs.
Roots, flesh red, centuries pale.
Hairsprings wound tight
Through fertile earthscapes
Where each layer feeds the next
Into depths immutable.
Though you must rise, must
Move large and slow
When it is time, O my
Gnarled mother-vine, ancient
As vanished ages,
Your spirit remains
Nourished,
Nourishing me.

I see your figure wrapped in skins
Curved into a mound of earth
Holding your rich dark roots.
Matmiya,
I see you sitting.

For Two Who Slipped Away Almost Entirely

Alice Walker

for two who
slipped away
almost
entirely:
my "part" Cherokee
great-grandmother
Tallulah
(Grandmama Lula)
on my mother's side
about whom
only one
agreed-upon
thing
is known:
her hair was so long
she could sit on it;

and my white (Anglo-Irish?)
great-great-grandfather
on my father's side;
nameless
(Walker, perhaps?),
whose only remembered act
is that he raped
a child:
my great-great-grandmother,
who bore his son,
my great-grandfather,
when she was eleven.

Rest in peace.
The meaning of your lives
is still
unfolding.

Rest in peace.
In me
the meaning of your lives
is still
unfolding.

Rest in peace, in me.
The meaning of your lives
is still
unfolding.

Rest. In me
the meaning of your lives
is still
unfolding.

Rest. In peace
in me
the meaning
of our lives
is still
unfolding.

Rest.

Legacies
Nikki Giovanni

her grandmother called her from the playground
    "yes, ma'am"
    "i want chu to learn how to make rolls," said the old
woman proudly
but the little girl didn't want
to learn how because she knew
even if she couldn't say it that
that would mean when the old one died she would be less
dependent on her spirit so
she said
    "i don't want to know how to make no rolls"
with her lips poked out
and the old woman wiped her hands on
her apron saying "lord
    these children"
and neither of them ever
said what they meant
and i guess nobody ever does

Whitecaps
Betsy Sholl

The bay is cold, heavy under a north wind.
Whitecaps keep coming. Little sheep,
the wind prods them along.
Waves of refugees, old people rocking.
My grandmother, her vision lost
in the hold of a ship, fingers
too numb to knit, though they never stop moving.

Is she a message the wind wants sent?
It brings tears to my eyes.
It cuts through my coat
till I'm naked as she was, hairless
between my legs.

I see her getting stripped:
Where were you born?
Her breasts sag like wet clothes on the line.
Can you read? Can you cook, sew?
No lice, literate. They pass her through.
Wind lulls, gusts. Cold and strong October.

Incredible sky. Piles of fleece.
She says, *Come, let's walk.*
Wind pulls at our voices, little kinks
of yarn the gulls snatch. She's 14,
about to board her first train.
Her father's hands cup her face and press
as if he could stop the noise, the steam,
the huge wheels beginning to roll.

Lineage
Margaret Walker

My grandmothers were strong.
They followed plows and bent to toil.
They moved through fields sowing seed.
They touched earth and grain grew.

They were full of sturdiness and singing.
My grandmothers were strong.

My grandmothers are full of memories
Smelling of soap and onions and wet clay
With veins rolling roughly over quick hands
They have many clean words to say.
My grandmothers were strong.
Why am I not as they?

Poem to My Grandmother in Her Death
Michele Murray

After a dozen years of death
even love wanders off, old faithful
dog tired of lying on stiff marble.

In any case you would not understand
this life, the plain white walls
& the books, a passion lost on you.

I do not know what forced your life
through iron years into a shape of giving—
an apple, squares of chocolate, a hand.

There should have been nothing left
after the mean streets, foaming washtubs,
the wild cries of births at home.

Never mind. It's crumbling in my hands,
too, what you gave. I've jumped from ledges
& landed oddly twisted, bleeding internally.

Thus I learn how to remember your injuries—
your sudden heaviness as fine rain fell,
or your silence over the scraped bread board.

Finding myself in the end is finding you
& if you are lost in the folds of your silence
then I find only to lose with you those years

I stupidly slung off me like ragged clothes
when I was ashamed to be the child
of your child. I scramble for them now

In dark closets because I am afraid.
I have forgotten so much. If I could meet you
again perhaps I could rejoin my own flesh

And not lose whatever you called love.
I could understand your silences & speak them
& you would be as present to me as your worn ring.

In the shadows I reach for the bucket of fierce dahlias
you bought without pricing, the coat you shook
free of its snow, the blouse that you ironed.

There's no love so pure it can thrive
without its incarnations. I would like to know you
once again over your chipped cups brimming with tea.

Five Poems for Grandmothers (excerpt)
Margaret Atwood

iii

How little I know
about you finally:

The time you stood
in the nineteenth century
on Yonge Street, a thousand
miles from home, with a brown purse
and a man stole it.

Six children, five who lived.
She never said anything
about those births and the one death;
her mouth closed on a pain
that could neither be told nor ignored.

She used to have such a sense of fun.
Now girls, she would say
when we would tease her.
Her anger though, why
that would curl your hair,
though she never swore.
The worst thing she could say was:
Don't be foolish.

At eighty she had two teeth pulled out
and walked the four miles home
in the noon sun, placing her feet
in her own hunched shadow.

The bibbed print aprons, the shock
of the red lace dress, the pin
I found at six in your second drawer,
made of white beads, the shape of a star.
What did we ever talk about
but food, health and the weather?

Sons branch out, but
one woman leads to another.
Finally I know you
through your daughters,
my mother, her sisters,
and through myself:

Is this you, this edgy joke
I make, are these your long fingers,
your hair of an untidy bird,
is this your outraged
eye, this grip
that will not give up?

Spring Fragments (excerpt)
Betsy Sholl

3
Dogwood blossoms, lovely and full—
how endangered they are. The forsythia shines
as if laughing to think it could ever fall
into the matronly hedge of summer.
The japonica's last buds just opened
this morning and already they tremble.

Apple and plum alone embrace every change
as if they had mothers who prepared them well,
from a gnarled wisdom teaching
there is a fruit that comes
when our first skirts are soiled
and fallen away.

4
I translate from the dreams of old women.
Drifting through lavender forests,
climbing with ease the yellow mountains
where you can lie down lost in forsythia—

coming to the end of spring
my grandmother kicks off her shoes,
steps out of her faltering body.

Prologue (excerpt)
Audre Lorde

The time of lamentation and curses is passing.

My mother survives now
through more than chance or token.
Although she will read what I write with embarrassment
or anger
and a small understanding
my children do not need to relive my past
in strength nor in confusion

nor care that their holy fires
may destroy
more than my failures

Somewhere in the landscape past noon
I shall leave a dark print
of the me that I am
and who I am not
etched in a shadow of angry and remembered loving
and their ghosts will move
whispering through them
with me none the wiser
for they will have buried me
either in shame
or in peace.

And the grasses will still be
Singing.

Poem at Thirty-nine
Alice Walker

How I miss my father.
I wish he had not been
so tired
when I was
born.

Writing deposit slips and checks
I think of him.
He taught me how.
This is the form,
he must have said:
the way it is done.
I learned to see
bits of paper
as a way
to escape
the life he knew
and even in high school
had a savings
account.

He taught me
that telling the truth
did not always mean
a beating;
though many of my truths
must have grieved him
before the end.

How I miss my father!
He cooked like a person
dancing
in a yoga meditation
and craved the voluptuous
sharing
of good food.

Now I look and cook just like him:
my brain light;
tossing this and that
into the pot;
seasoning none of my life
the same way twice; happy to feed
whoever strays my way.

He would have grown
to admire
the woman I've become:
cooking, writing, chopping wood,
staring into the fire.

The Envelope
Maxine Kumin

It is true, Martin Heidegger, as you have written,
I fear to cease, even knowing that at the hour
of my death my daughters will absorb me, even
knowing they will carry me about forever
inside them, an arrested fetus, even as I carry
the ghost of my mother under my navel, a nervy
little androgynous person, a miracle
folded in lotus position.

Like those old pear-shaped Russian dolls that open
at the middle to reveal another and another, down
to the pea-sized, irreducible minim,
may we carry our mothers forth in our bellies.
May we, borne onward by our daughters, ride
in the Envelope of Almost-Infinity,
that chain letter good for the next twenty-five
thousand days of their lives.

Eggs
Sharon Olds

My daughter has turned against eggs. Age six
to nine, she cooked them herself, getting up
at six to crack the shells, slide the
three yolks into the bowl,
slit them with the whisk, beat them till they hissed
and watch the pan like an incubator as they
firmed, gold. Lately she's gone from
three to two to one and now she
cries she wants to quit eggs.
It gets on her hands, it's slimy, and it's hard
to get all the little things out:
puddles of gluten glisten on the counter
with small, curled shapes floating in their
sexual smear. She moans. It is getting
too close. Next birthday she's ten and then
it's open season, no telling when
the bright, crimson dot appears
like the sign on a fertilized yolk. She has carried
all her eggs in the two baskets
woven into her fine side,
but soon they'll be slipping down gently,
sliding. She grips the counter where the raw
whites jump, and the spiral shapes
signal from the glittering gelatine, and she
wails for her life.

The Moment
Sharon Olds

When I saw the dark Egyptian stain,
I went down into the house to find you, Mother—
past the grandfather clock, with its huge
ochre moon, past the burnt
sienna woodwork, rubbed and glazed.
I went deeper and deeper down into the
body of the house, down below the
level of the earth. It must have been
the maid's day off, for I found you there
where I had never found you, by the wash tubs,
your hands thrust deep in soapy water,
and above your head, the blazing windows
at the surface of the ground.
You looked up from the iron sink,
a small haggard pretty woman
of 40, one week divorced.
"I've got my period, Mom," I said,
and saw your face abruptly break open and
glow with joy. "Baby," you said,
coming toward me, hands out and
covered with tiny delicate bubbles like seeds.

Three Sweatshop Women
Nanying Stella Wong

the yardage flows. . .

in the arc of white light
eyes untangle threads of necessity,
needling the cloth as centuries-skilled
hands feed the machines.
a Chungsahn woman declares.
"these stripes bring my dead eyes alive!"
and makes her machine sing . . .
"another piece—three dozen,
money to send old ma to buy ginseng"

perched on high stool—one from
village of Toisahn snaps scissors
in porcelain hands   closed
like jaws of the shark—
she was here looking for new world long ago. . .
"one day my mirror showed me my white head!
looking now for what world?
only cut-cut-cut, pattern after pattern. . . "

the small lady, turning, half-smiles. .
she sees a carp in autumn petals, leaves,
the water of her years she has swallowed—
her children   they can leap to higher waters!
become chemist, doctor, engineer. . .
she leans to her iron, press-smooths
each piece in steam of purpose—
the long cord trails to her timing

the garments grow . . .

A Poem about Faith
Kathleen Norris

My face is Mrs. Heyward's,
Long and thin. In the photograph I have of her
She is sending a son
To the Great War. Her mother,
A mill-owner's daughter from Manchester,
Was disowned for running to America
With a Methodist.

I wear Mrs. Hutton's wedding ring:
It's washed countless dishes
At church suppers,
And pulled white shirts
Through a steam-hot wringer.
I have her daughter's fine bones,
My grandmother Totten.
But I'll be stooped like grandmother Norris
When I'm old, with alert eyes:

And while I may never have her faith in Jesus,
At the end, like her,
I know I'll expect to see my mother.

I have no photograph
Of the milliner, a second cousin
Who wed a doctor
Against advice.
She ran away, and the police found her
In Chicago:
She'd bought netting and feathers,
But couldn't remember her name.

Or the girl raped at Bible Camp
By an old preacher, who spoke gently
As he lifted her skirts
And slid his hands
Up her ten-year-old legs.
She sailed for Africa, and mission work,
When I was a child.

I have a scratched recording
Of another aunt, singing hymns
In a rich soprano.
She heard the voices
Of the lost tribes of Israel,
But her own voice led her
Into temptation, and she seduced
A farm boy from the church choir.

She jumped out a window
At the state hospital
The year I was born,
And I want more than anything
To know she has been forgiven.

the will's love
Besmilr Brigham

love God—
           my mother said
He who shut the Lion's mouth
and sealed the flames to their own burning

"the soul is like a little bird in His hand
a bird that lives in a wild briar tree"

love Life—my father said
laying the map out
        green-red mountains
        blue-yellow sea
the soul is a migrant
roc-bird that nests on sea rocks
a hawk   a falcon—
              an eagle
or a "splatter-wing parrot
that only at night sleeps in a tree"

it took
my childhood before I could see

each one
said the same
        I am

          love me

What Is Repeated, What Abides
Barbara Hendryson

The light of the moon illumines only
the highest trees. Beyond that, repetitions
of darkness: the trees darker than darkness
and a deeper blackness passing among them.

And hours from now, the crack of bird-
song, small scurryings among
the leaves, a high pitched cry.
In the open, beyond the forest, light

in the sea. Light in the dewless grass.
Light in the stone. Only the moon
knows what is repeated, what abides—
among these, the continuous tides of the water,

a man casting his nets,
a woman gathering salt.

Elegy
Maya Angelou

for Harriet Tubman & Frederick Douglass

I lay down in my grave
and watch my children
grow
Proud blooms
above the weeds of death.

Their petals wave
and still nobody
knows the soft black
dirt that is my winding
sheet. The worms, my friends,
yet tunnel holes in
bones and through those
apertures I see the rain.
The sunfelt warmth
now jabs
within my space and
brings me roots of my
children born.

Their seeds must fall
and press beneath
this earth,

and find me where I
wait. My only need to
fertilize their birth.

I lay down in my grave
and watch my children
grow.

Death and Lesser Losses

No book treating matters of the spirit can fail to make loss and death a central theme, for tragedy challenges each of us to reconcile faith with fate. In this section the reader will find poems about abortion, miscarriage, and suicide, as well as more conventional selections about death. Pain and grieving are expressed openly and directly, in a manner that brings cleansing power. I have chosen to include selections on aging in this section as well, for the loss of physical powers is one that we feel keenly. And yet aging is not presented for the most part as something to fear; rather it is a ripening, a relinquishment made with dignity and trust.

The Mother

Gwendolyn Brooks

Abortions will not let you forget.
You remember the children you got that you did not get,
The damp small pulps with a little or with no hair,
The singers and workers that never handled the air.
You will never neglect or beat
Them, or silence or buy with a sweet.
You will never wind up the sucking-thumb
Or scuttle off ghosts that come.
You will never leave them, controlling your luscious sigh,
Return for a snack of them, with gobbling mother-eye.

I have heard in the voices of the wind the voices of my dim killed
    children.
I have contracted. I have eased
My dim dears at the breasts they could never suck.
I have said, Sweets, if I sinned, if I seized
Your luck
And your lives from your unfinished reach,
If I stole your births and your names,
Your straight baby tears and your games,
Your stilted or lovely loves, your tumults, your marriages, aches, and
    your deaths,
If I poisoned the beginnings of your breaths,
Believe that even in my deliberateness I was not deliberate.
Though why should I whine,
Whine that the crime was other than mine?—
Since anyhow you are dead.
Or rather, or instead,
You were never made.
But that too, I am afraid,
Is faulty: oh, what shall I say, how is the truth to be said?
You were born, you had body, you died.
It is just that you never giggled or planned or cried.

Believe me, I loved you all.
Believe me, I knew you, though faintly, and I loved, I loved you
All.

ten years ago
Eileen Moeller

had you been born
I would have stayed a child
squinting through my mother's
steamy windows, barely visible
over the sill

instead I did what the rabbits do
in a drought
dissolved you with dread and fear
back into timelessness
your life no more than a startle
for both of us
a breeze rearranging everything
before it goes

little tadpole
gone back to the ghostworld
I went to the crossroads
could go no further
could go no further
left you as fine as a mustache hair
on your father's soft lipped mouth
saying no
ten years ago
I bled on a white padded table
and the crone sang her black song

and here I am now
still carrying you
a question mark curled asleep
in the keening dark of my mouth
a seed unspoken
you rise
pearl in the moon of my thumbnail
tiny mirror
I am still bleeding

Unborn Child Elegy (excerpt)
Margaret Gibson

Today snow sparks the air like mica—the sun's
just so, cocked right angles to the wind.
I bring you the snow and it isn't enough.
You whisper you want to be born.

I study your whisper, I study my fear.
You're bound, my mother said, to pain.
Each child pries you open.

No one will believe
how alive and present to me you are if I refuse
you a body. But I believe in nothing, a transparent
breath from which all form and color rise
in a passion of wings and leaves.

In the ancient stories, the world begins by surprise
when zero speaks, from mere words
weaving sun and moon, the fire
the flash of snow.

Be the zero who speaks for me.
Be birth and death, the emptiness
only a child, and never a child, can fill.

Country Woman Elegy
Margaret Gibson

With a hush in their voices
country people round here tell of the woman who walked
bareheaded in winter, keening aloud,
three days wandering with her seven-month child
dead inside her. She wouldn't be comforted,
she held her loss.

Telling this
the old men shake fear from their eyes as they might
shake rain from a hat or coat. Her madness they blame
on winter, the cold and closed-in weather.

I love that woman's fearless
mourning. The child dead, no help for that,
she had to wait until her wanting to love the child
died out in echo and outcry against bare stone.
She had to walk, nevermind the cold,
until she learned what she needed
to learn, letting go.

And I love those reticent men.
They know how most of us strain to ignore our dead,
the woman less fortunate to feel the weight of hers.
Who wants to admit death's there inside, more privy
to our secrets than any lover, and love
a kind of grief?

Therefore we dream.
Last night a wild, purple bougainvillea bloomed in sleep.
I thought to gather a handful, but the stalks broke
like straws, and the wind
took them

and drove them past that woman
bareheaded on the winter road, that woman whose cries
unwound and wouldn't be comforted by love or a lover's body,
by childhood or any piety.

Flowers

Kathleen Fraser

Changing water. Adding aspirin. Nitrogen, potash or
sugar (white) to keep limpness from descending upon
these purple and magenta asters with broad golden centers
and petals packed in two rows making fringe above
green spread leaves, still alive. Keep cutting stems
to retain the vertical pull of water up into
the barely charged life.

She said there was a tiny charge of energy still, like a cord, moving between
me and the child—a girl—though its body life had stopped after four
months, only one leg intact on the fetus. "It's better," the doctor said. "Nature
knows best," he said, at the end.

That was ten years ago. He was pulling me along on an immaculate silver
table, larger than a serving tray, I thought, sheet over me then, white linen,
and their faces soothing. Shapes of words and eyes. I couldn't identify. Something inside me had broken, though I tried to hold it in. Red, on everything.

> In the white stone pitcher I always place flowers.
> First water, then the spiked metal frog
> where each flower is stuck in arrangements of
> height, darkness or intensity of bloom. The accidents
> interest me. The Japanese effect of less.
> Space showing its wandering shape between leaves
> and the sudden curve of a stem
> dying slowly towards what light is
> in the room. One forgets about hunger,
> absorbed in the fuschia and the mauve.

104.

Alta

> what shall i wear
> to suffer my third miscarriage?
> something appealing but not sexy.
> i never want to look sexy anymore;
> not if i have to step outside my home.
>
> (for the visit to the doctor
> i wore a red skirt / blood
> on blood-red, who would notice?
> & tucked my shirt in, to reveal
> my fetchingly flat belly /
> but everyone knew i was bleeding
> anyway, the tears wouldn't stop.)

3 : 1

Alta

but with the steady ache that knowledge carves in us,
where can we go?
—michael mc clure

suicide is such a bore. one wishes one's friends would stop it.
how can we have visions & cure the world when our friends
are dropping like flies? how can we know which friends we
must see this week so that they wont do themselves in? it's
just exhausting.

plus, one never knows if a timely phone call could have saved
them anyway. maybe you would have made the phone call,
& felt loving & felt happy to talk to them (even if they were
sad) & they would have put down the phone, walked into the
garage, & started the engine anyway. then one really *would*
feel awful. at any rate, i wish they'd quit. i spend probably
a solid week crying, when i could be out dancing or making
t.v. shows. one wishes they would call first. & then perhaps
both of us could go out dancing.

but the point of suicide is, of course, that there is no one to
call. not even if we really are there.

My Grandfather
Joanne Hotchkiss

The coiled asp
of suicide I carry
goes back to my grandfather
who hung himself from a punching bag
in the attic,
and co-incides with me, his namesake,
my guilt bent as simply as a figure
constructed of hairpins.
My grandfather, a small man
was named for the Biblical Joseph
who saved his life
by interpreting dreams.

Suicide is one of my roots
and in order to redeem myself,
I seem condemned to turn other spirits
from that rope: steps to the attic
like slots where suicides reach
their wires beneath living
deadly house-ghosts,
the addicts swinging through voluptuous
shadows swallowing the light.

I enter this defeat with my hands
tied up in prayers.
The old paths lead me back
as I try to interpret this dream
walking through walls and no matter
how many times they close
I have to keep pushing
and pushing them open.

Lynn
Jeanne Foster

I have been thinking
of sleeping
like my cousin, beneath
the sweet dark needles
of the pine that sings
to her day and night
day and night, so that

even now she is not alone.
It is like that, you know.

If an angel
friend is with you
when your heart goes out
between your ribs,
you will never again suffer loneliness.
If a half-smile is on your lips,
you will remember the old pain,
but it is forever
mitigated.

Lynn
saw the silver animals
in the cumulus clouds
transforming themselves.
Her gaze
rested upon the steps
of the falling building, stone by stone
becoming one with nature.
She travelled back down
the backwoods road, thirty-five miles
to Pensacola and along the coast
to her mother's house. She stayed awhile
with her mother's face. Moved

by breeze, shadows of pine
stroked her cheek,
moments of light flickered
upon her lids. The singing
brought her home again. Her eyes

opened one last time, she half-smiled
and left behind her the pill jars
and the empty bottle of wine. The pine
stood over her five nights
five days. When the officer
in uniform finally came
to look through her car window,

she was above, among the sweet dark needles.

Easter, 1968

May Sarton

Now we have buried the face we never knew,
Now we have silenced the voice we never heard,
Now he is dead we look on him with awe . . .
Dead king, dear martyr, and anointed Word.
Where thousands followed, each must go home
Into his secret heart and learn the pain,
Stand there on rock and, utterly alone,
Come to terms with this burning suffering man;

Torn by his hunger from our fat and greed,
And bitten by his thirst from careless sloth,
Must wake, inflamed, to answer for his blood
With the slow-moving inexorable truth
That we can earn even a moment's balm
Only with acts of caring, and fierce calm.

Head of an African, vital and young,
The full lips fervent as an open rose,
The high-domed forehead full of light and strong—
Look on this man again. The blood still flows.
Listen once more to the impassioned voice
Till we are lifted on his golden throat
And trumpet-call of agony and choice
One of our hesitating shame and doubt.
Remember how he prayed before the task.
Remember how he walked, eyes bright and still,
Unarmed, his bronze face shining like a mask,
Through stones and curses, hatred hard as hail.
Now we have silenced the voice we never heard,
Break open, heart, and listen to his word.

What Hell Is

Heather McHugh

March, 1985

Your father sits inside
his spacious kitchen, corpulent
and powerless. Nobody knows
how your disease is spread; it came
from love, or some
such place. Your father's bought
with forty years of fast talk, door-to-door,
this fancy house you've come home now to die in.
Let me tell you what
hell is, he says: I got this
double fridge all full of food
and I can't let my son go in.

*

Your parents' friends
stop visiting. You are a damper on
their spirits. Every day you feel
more cold (no human being
here can bear
the thought—it's growing
huge, as you grow thin).
Ain't it a bitch, you say, this
getting old? (I'm not sure
I should laugh. No human being
helps, except
suddenly, simply
Jesus: him you hold.)

*

We're not allowed
to touch you if you weep or bleed.
Applying salve to sores that cannot heal
your brother wears a rubber glove.
With equal meaning, cold or kiss
could kill you. Now what do I mean
by love?

*

The man who used
to love his looks
is sunk in bone
and looking out.

Framed by immunities
of telephone and lamp
his mouth is shut,
his eyes are dark.

While we discuss despair
he is it, somewhere
in the house. Increasingly
he's spoken of

not with. In kitchen
conferences we come
to terms that we
can bear. But where is he?

In hell, which is
the living room.
In hell, which has
an easy chair.

Mama Rosanna's Last Bead-Clack
Laurel Speer

I'm sitting on my couch saying my rosary. I haven't
been inside a Catholic church in 14 years, but this
is something I learned early and gave up never.
It's my ritual when I wake up choking. I drink hot tea;
I don't take in food; I listen; I say my decades;
I pray; I look at TV. My color isn't good; I'm losing
weight; my lungs fill up. I'm old; I'm used up;
I haven't lived a good life. I don't go out;
I don't wash. I've seen pictures on TV and know now
I'm one of them. I'm afraid. People will come
to my house and burn my bedding. Lamb of God, kill me.

Lament
Edna St. Vincent Millay

Listen, children:
Your father is dead.
From his old coats
I'll make you little jackets;
I'll make you little trousers
From his old pants.
There'll be in his pockets
Things he used to put there,
Keys and pennies
Covered with tobacco;
Dan shall have the pennies
To save in his bank;
Anne shall have the keys

To make a pretty noise with.
Life must go on,
And the dead be forgotten;
Life must go on,
Though good men die;
Anne, eat your breakfast;
Dan, take your medicine;
Life must go on;
I forget just why.

"Goodnight, Willie Lee, I'll See You in the Morning"
Alice Walker

Looking down into my father's
dead face
for the last time
my mother said without
tears, without smiles
without regrets
but with *civility*
"Goodnight, Willie Lee, I'll see you
in the morning."
And it was then I knew that the healing
of all our wounds
is forgiveness
that permits a promise
of our return
at the end.

Finding the Lamb (*excerpt*)
Rebecca Newth

I had gone out to check on new lambs
at night, and been scared
by the skimming air
and by the deep stars shining overhead

(wireless lights sank and flashed,
and the chickens slept in their reptilian
way) and found the lamb sleeping
on the January ground

and, finding the lamb well, I wished to die
because the night had kept a child
of mine, the great black night
and the new day as well.

Aunt Lucy
Jane Gentry

As pure at ninety-four as any babe
new born, Aunt Lucy died. She loved
a maiden's pleasures: purple, funerals,
young company, blooming hats, Jesus.
At Easter church, without an orchid
to her name, she would survey
the flowering bosoms and chastely
dream a dark-dyed purple of her own.

In Lucy's bright-eyed, backward mind,
eighty years ago was near as now: jigging
through lamplight into daylight, she frisked
her mare daylong, outrode her posting,
untied beaux, until she galloped her cane to bed,
vowing she wouldn't last through winter.

Now that stones are cold, trees naked,
gardens brittle, she sleeps like a baby,
clutching a queer blossom, trundled away
under the beds of tulips and the plots of daffodils,
tucked in beneath the blanket of snow
where bulbs smolder between sheets of ice.

Planted with her first and only orchid,
Lucy winters through, her old maid mind,
feeble as February sun, recollecting snow.
Let her hold out for some combustion of that bloom
whose shoots may yet fire spring

when the cold comforter melts—
her and her rootless flower.
For they lie here and, under cover of death,
sleep a short sleep.

Apples
Shirley Kaufman

No use waiting for it to stop
raining in my face like a wet towel,
having to catch a plane,
to pick the apples from her tree
and bring them home.

The safest place to be
is under the branches. She
in her bed and her mouth
dry in the dry room.
Don't go out in the rain.

I stretch my arms for apples
anyway, feel how the ripe ones
slide in my hands like cups
that want to be perfect. Juices
locked up in the skin.

She used to slice them in quarters,
cut through the core,
open the inside out. Fingers
steady on the knife, expert
at stripping things.

Sometimes she split them sideways
into halves to let a star break
from the center with tight seeds,
because I wanted that,
six petals in the flesh.

Flavor of apples inhaled as flowers,
not even biting them.
Apples at lunch or after school
like soup, a fragrance rising
in the steam, eat and be well.

In the House of the Dying
Jane Cooper

So once again, hearing the tired aunts
whisper together under the kitchen globe,
I turn away; I am not one of them.

At the sink I watch the water cover my hands
in a sheath of light. Upstairs she lies alone
dreaming of autumn nights when her children were born.

On the steps between us grows in a hush of waiting
the impossible silence between two generations.
The aunts buzz on like flies around a bulb.

I am dressed like them. Standing with my back turned
I wash the dishes in the same easy way.
Only at birth and death do I utterly fail.

For death is my old friend who waits on the stairs.
Whenever I pass I nod to him like the newsman
who is there every day; for them he is the priest.

While the birth of love is so terrible to me
I feel unworthy of the commonest marriage.
Upstairs she lies, washed through by the two miracles.

In Flight

Jennifer Regan

The Whisperjet swings wildly
From one air pocket to another
As I fly to bury you.

Is it you, jostling the plane,
Making sure you have the last word?

We dip into shadow. I feel
Your loss as if my own vital signs
Were failing. The plane steadies.
Light floods the window.

I search the sky for something
Familiar, a Sunday School scene
Colored too bright, a figure
Soaring against all gravity and sense

And think I see you rise
From a white cloud that spirals
Off the tail—my brother
Leaping like a boy who believes

He can fly. One arm beckons,
The other is beating like a wing.

Grandmother

Marilyn Krysl

I wasn't there when your body, signaling, woke you
When you sat, moving yourself to the edge, and stood
and knew July by its heat and wondered what time it was
and steadied yourself, sat down, and called out for my mother

When she came, her impatience visible in the air around her
because it was hot and something in a pot needed stirring
When she helped you into the slip worn thin by your patience
When she asked which dress you wanted to wear

and when you pulled on the stockings yourself, and the garters
and stepped into your shoes and looked down and knew
and did not tell my mother you knew
When you asked her please would she comb your hair

When you sat down to the meal with my mother and father
and my father asked *would you like some of this   and some of this*
When you lifted the glass and gazed through the water's prism
When you drank, swallow by swallow, all of the water

and opened the napkin but did not pick up the fork
When you folded the napkin and pushed back the plate,
pushed back the chair and stood with no help from anyone
and turned, saying nothing, and walked out of the room

When they called you   When you did not answer
When you shut the door and looked at your face in the mirror
Your face   that friend of long standing, that trustworthy sister
When you took this face in your hands to bid it goodby

and when you said to them *I want to lie down now*
When they laid you down and covered you with a sheet
and you said *Go on now, go eat* and they did
because they had worked and were hungry and this had happened
     before

When you lay back in it to let it have you
knowing what you had waited for patiently and impatiently
what you had longed and hoped for and abandoned longing and
     hoping for
and prayed for and not received was finally here

When you lay back in it to let it have you
When you heard for the last time the clink of silver
and let go the sheet, let go light on the earth
When your breath ceased to be a thing that belonged to you

I wasn't there
Forgive me
I wasn't there

Betrothed
Louise Bogan

You have put your two hands upon me, and your mouth,
You have said my name as a prayer.
Here where trees are planted by the water
I have watched your eyes, cleansed from regret,
And your lips, closed over all that love cannot say.

My mother remembers the agony of her womb
And long years that seemed to promise more than this.
She says, "You do not love me,
You do not want me,
You will go away."

In the country whereto I go
I shall not see the face of my friend
Nor her hair the color of sunburnt grasses;
Together we shall not find
The land on whose hills bends the new moon
In air traversed of birds.

What have I thought of love?
I have said, "It is beauty and sorrow."
I have thought that it would bring me lost delights, and splendor
As a wind out of old time. . . .

But there is only the evening here,
And the sound of willows
Now and again dipping their long oval leaves in the water.

Some Slippery Afternoon
Daniela Gioseffi

A silver watch you've worn for years
is suddenly gone
leaving a pale white stripe
blazing on your wrist.

A calendar in which you've marked all the appointments
you've kept
(or meant to keep)
disappears
leaving a faded spot on the wall
where it hung.
You search the house and yard and trash cans for weeks
and never find it.

One night the glass in your windows
vanishes
leaving you sitting in a gust of wind.

You think how a leg is suddenly lost
beneath a subway train
or a taxi wheel
some slippery afternoon.

The child you've raised for years
combing each lock,
tailoring each smile, each tear,
each valuable thought,
suddenly metamorphoses into a harlequin
and joins the circus passing in the street
never to be seen again.

One morning you wash your face,
look into the mirror,
and find the water has eroded your features,
worn them smooth as a rock in a brook.
A blank oval peers back at you
too mouthless to cry out
for what has suddenly gone.

Gift from the Sea (excerpt)
Anne Morrow Lindbergh

Intermittency—an impossible lesson for human beings to learn. How can one learn to live through the ebb-tides of one's existence? How can one learn to take the trough of the wave? It is easier to understand here on the beach, where the breathlessly still ebb-tides reveal another life below the level which mortals usually reach. In this crystalline moment of suspense, one has a sudden revelation of the secret kingdom at the bottom of the sea. Here in the shallow flats one finds, wading through warm ripples, great horse-conchs pivoting on a leg; white sand dollars, marble medallions engraved in the mud; and myriads of bright-colored cochina-clams, glistening in the foam, their shells opening and shutting like butterflies' wings. So beautiful is the still hour of the sea's withdrawal, as beautiful as the sea's return when the encroaching waves pound up the beach, pressing to reach those dark rumpled chains of seaweed which mark the last high tide.

Perhaps this is the most important thing for me to take back from beach-living: simply the memory that each cycle of the tide is valid; each cycle of the wave is valid; each cycle of a relationship is valid. And my shells? I can sweep them all into my pocket. They are only there to remind me that the sea recedes and returns eternally.

Waiting
Jane Cooper

My body knows it will never bear children.
What can I say to my body now,
this used violin?
Every night it cries out strenuously
from its secret cave.

Old body, old friend,
why are you so unforgiving?

Why are you so stiff and resistant
clenched around empty space?
An instrument is not a box.

But suppose you are an empty box?
Suppose you are like that famous wooden music hall in Troy, New York,
waiting to be torn down
where the orchestras love to play?

Let compassion breathe in and out of you,
filling you
and singing

The Cancer Journals (excerpt)

Audre Lorde

In a perspective of urgency, I want to say now that I'd give anything to have done it differently—it being the birth of a unique and survival-worthy, or survival-effective, perspective. Or I'd give anything not to have cancer and my beautiful breast gone, fled with my love of it. But then immediately after I guess I have to qualify that—there really are some things I wouldn't give. I wouldn't give my life, first of all, or else I wouldn't have chosen to have the operation in the first place, and I did. I wouldn't give Frances, or the children, or even any one of the women I love. I wouldn't give up my poetry, and I guess when I come right down to it I wouldn't give my eyes, nor my arms. So I guess I do have to be careful that my urgencies reflect my priorities.

Sometimes I feel like I'm the spoils in a battle between good and evil, right now, or that I'm both sides doing the fighting, and I'm not even sure of the outcome nor the terms. But sometimes it comes into my head, like right now, what would you really give? And it feels like, even just musing, I could make a terrible and tragic error of judgement if I don't always keep my head and my priorities clear. It's as if the devil is really trying to buy my soul, and pretending that it doesn't matter if I say yes because everybody knows he's not for real anyway. But I don't know that. And I don't think this is all a dream at all, and no, I would not give up love.

Maybe this is the chance to live and speak those things I really do believe, that power comes from moving into whatever I fear most that cannot be avoided. But will I ever be strong enough again to open my mouth and not have a cry of raw pain leap out?

Gestalt at Sixty (excerpt)

May Sarton

> I am not ready to die,
> But I am learning to trust death
> As I have trusted life.
> I am moving
> Toward a new freedom
> Born of detachment,
> And a sweeter grace—
> Learning to let go.

I am not ready to die,
But as I approach sixty
I turn my face toward the sea.
I shall go where tides replace time,
Where my world will open to a far horizon
Over the floating, never-still flux and change.
I shall go with the changes,
I shall look far out over golden grasses
And blue waters. . . .

There are no farewells.

Praise God for His mercies,
For His austere demands,
For His light
And for His darkness.

Ebba Dawson: Mardel Rest Home, Haskell, New Jersey

Maria Gillan

Ebba sits at the window
patiently waiting
for the few minutes
I can give.

With her, I see all the others
trapped in monastic rooms,
rooms stamped with trophies
that shout I am loved,
pictures
of grandchildren tucked
in cheap dresser
mirrors, Christmas cards propped
on plastic doilies though the forsythia
already blooms.

Ebba balances metal canes
down brown-carpeted
stairs, trembles as we enter
the restaurant, is pleased by Lipton tea.

I touch her hand, the skin almost translucent
and threaded with lines like fish swimming toward
the river's mouth.

I bow to that which remains
in us, resilient,
unbroken, our greed for life
leaping
against all odds.

The Measure of My Days (excerpt)
Florida Scott-Maxwell

Another secret [the elderly] carry is that though drab outside—wreckage to
the eye, mirrors a mortification—inside we flame with a wild life that is almost incommunicable. In silent, hot rebellion we cry silently—"I have lived
my life haven't I? What more is expected of me?" Have we got to pretend out
of noblesse oblige that age is nothing, in order to encourage the others? This
we do with a certain haughtiness, realising now that we have reached the
place beyond resignation, a place I had no idea existed until I had arrived here.

It is a place of fierce energy. Perhaps passion would be a better word than
energy, for the sad fact is this vivid life cannot be used. If I try to transpose it
into action I am soon spent. It has to be accepted as passionate life, perhaps
the life I never lived, never guessed I had it in me to live. It feels other and
more than that. It feels like the far side of precept and aim. It is just life, the
natural intensity of life, and when old we have it for our reward and undoing.
It can—at moments—feel as though we had it for our glory. Some of it must
go beyond good and bad, for at times—though this comes rarely, unexpect-
edly—it is a swelling clarity as though all was resolved. It has no content, it
seems to expand us, it does not derive from the body, and then it is gone. It
may be a degree of consciousness which lies outside activity, and which when
young we are too busy to experience.

Testimony
Jane Flanders

This is how death
came to the old tree:
in a cold bolt, a single
thrust from a cloud,
in a tearing away of bark
and limbs, a piercing
of much that was necessary.

We had no choice then
but to cut it down—a pine
of great height, that knew much
about weather and small life.
It had been here longer
than any of us. And now
there is a hole in the sky.

Planting Onions
Jane Flanders

It is right
that I fall to my knees
on this damp, stony cake,
that I bend my back
and bow my head.

Sun warms my shoulders,
the nape of my neck,
and the air is tangy with rot.
Bulbs rustle like spirits
in their sack.

I bury each one
a trowel's width under.
May they take hold,
rising green in time
to help us weep and live.

Survivors
Chana Bloch

And then she died and became
available to us. Piled outside the city
with the others, hubcap and fender. We are slowly
stripping her.

"She wanted the doctor
to tell her." We sit
in a circle with our shoes off. The silky
feel of her secrets. "She wanted
a child. She even—."
The dead are the property of the living.

But did she know?
I rubbed her shoulders with cologne
on a wad of cotton.
She asked for that. Head on the pillow, heavy, the iron
edge of the bed.
She had a few wishes left then, each one
smaller than the last.

"Tell me." And she stared
through the spotted
double-glazed panes. "What I want."

We live like survivors in a barren country.
We take what we need.

The Poem as a Reservoir for Grief (excerpt)
Tess Gallagher

It is important that we be strengthened by the wisdom of our grievings. The
scientists may tinker, the politicians may instruct us in the various ploys of
unconsciousness, the physicians may delay death awhile with yet another
cure, but, until each individual maintains a responsible relationship to his or
her own losses and changes, there will be no such thing as a hopeful future.
For, as in the Taoist description of the wheel in terms of the strong, empty

spaces *between* the spokes, one's future depends not only on the visible spokes of the present, but also on those invisible elements from the past, those things we are missing, are grieving for, have forgotten and left behind, so that they may be recovered.

In the Midst of Winter (excerpt)
Mary Jane Moffat

At a recent exhibit of American quilts at the Oakland Art Museum I was moved by an example titled "Widow's Quilt." The artist had fashioned from her husband's clothes a tableau of their life together. Around certain scenes—their wedding day, the gravestone of a child—her usually meticulous patching veered, the uneven stitches a powerful metaphor for her grief. By assembling from the fabric of memory all that had been lost, all she still cherished, she created a comforter of warmth for others and a work of enduring beauty. The quiltmaker . . . suggest[s] that each of us might create, in our own way, something new from sorrow.

In Blackwater Woods
Mary Oliver

Look, the trees
are turning
their own bodies
into pillars

of light,
are giving off the rich
fragrance of cinnamon
and fulfillment,

the long tapers
of cattails
are bursting and floating away over
the blue shoulders

of the ponds,
and every pond,
no matter what its
name is, is

nameless now.
Every year
everything
I have ever learned

in my lifetime
leads back to this: the fires
and the black river of loss
whose other side

is salvation,
whose meaning
none of us will ever know.
To live in this world

you must be able
to do three things:
to love what is mortal;
to hold it

against your bones knowing
your own life depends on it;
and, when the time comes to let it go,
to let it go.

Anxiety about Dying
Alicia Ostriker

It isn't any worse than what
I discover in the dentist's chair
Under the nitrous oxide.

The whole jaw is going, I complain, the gums, the bone,
Two enormous fillings just last week. What do I need?
How about a guillotine, says my dentist, the joker.

The only thing I have to fear is fear itself, I tell him.
You believe in that bullshit? he says,
Setting to work on my rotting bicuspid.

Now comes the good part. Breathing the happy gas
I get answers to all the questions I had
About death but was afraid to ask.

Will there be pain? Yes.
Will my desires still be unsatisfied? Yes.
My human potential still unrealized? Yes.

Can a person stop minding about that? Certainly.
Can I commend my spirit to the seventeen
Angels whistling outside the dentist's window?

Of course. How nice the happy gas.
What a good friend.
I unclench my sweaty little hand.

I wave goodbye to my teeth.
It seems they are leaving by train for a vacation.
I'll meet them in the country when I can.

Sonnet 2 from "The Autumn Sonnets"
May Sarton

If I can let you go as trees let go
Their leaves, so casually, one by one;
If I can come to know what they do know,
That fall is the release, the consummation,
Then fear of time and the uncertain fruit
Would not distemper the great lucid skies
This strangest autumn, mellow and acute.
If I can take the dark with open eyes
And call it seasonal, not harsh or strange
(For love itself may need a time of sleep),
And, treelike, stand unmoved before the change,
Lose what I lose to keep what I can keep,
The strong root still alive under the snow,
Love will endure—if I can let you go.

All Souls

May Sarton

Did someone say that there would be an end,
An end, Oh, an end, to love and mourning?
Such voices speak when sleep and waking blend,
The cold bleak voices of the early morning
When all the birds are dumb in dark November—
Remember and forget, forget, remember.

After the false night, warm true voices, wake!
Voice of the dead that touches the cold living,
Through the pale sunlight once more gravely speak.
Tell me again, while the last leaves are falling:
"Dear child, what has been once so interwoven
Cannot be raveled, nor the gift ungiven."

Now the dead move through all of us still glowing,
Mother and child, lover and lover mated,
Are wound and bound together and enflowing.
What has been plaited cannot be unplaited—
Only the strands grow richer with each loss
And memory makes kings and queens of us.

Dark into light, light into darkness, spin.
When all the birds have flown to some real haven,
We who find shelter in the warmth within,
Listen, and feel new-cherished, new-forgiven,
As the lost human voices speak through us and blend
Our complex love, our mourning without end.

Songs of Brokenness and Alienation

Division, distrust, physical and economic violence—our country is not as we would wish it to be. The selections in this section acknowledge the spiritual sickness in our culture and at the same time imply that a better way is possible. Themes include racism, sexism, poverty, homelessness, divorce, abuse, and rape.

Crazy Quilt

Jane Wilson Joyce

The Liberty Bell in Philadelphia
is cracked. California is splitting
off. There is no East or West, no rhyme,
no reason to it. We are scattered.

Dear Lord, lest we all be somewhere
else, patch this work. Quilt us
together, feather-stitching piece
by piece our tag-ends of living,
our individual scraps of love.

Silence. She Is Six Years Old

Lynn Emanuel

She sleeps on a cot in the living room.
This is her father's mother's house.
And in the kitchen the men run their knife blades
across the oilcloth with roses on the table
and grandmother cooks them steak and eggs.
She is pretending to be asleep but she is listening
to the men talking about their friends
and grandmother in her white dress
walks back and forth past the door
and a hand reaches for salt and water.
Her father talks about divorce.
Now it is quiet.
Grandmother has left, her tight stockings
showed rainbows
and someone's upstairs undressing,
his dog tags making faint noise.
Her father walks into the room.
He is naked and there are certain
parts of him that are shadows.
And he pulls the blankets to the floor
and then the sheet—as if not to wake her—
and he lifts her up and whispers his wife's name—
Rachel, Rachel

and he takes her hand, small with its clean nails,
and he puts it to the dark:
Oh Rae, Oh Rachel he says
and over his shoulder she can see
the long hall mirror framed in black wood
and she smells lavender in her father's hair
when he gets up, first only his hands
and knees like someone playing horse,
and puts her on the chair
and she sits and rocks like a deaf woman.

Greg's Got Custody of Sally
Julia Alvarez

Greg's got custody of Sally and wants
to fall in love with a stepmother so
Sally can have a mommie like her friends
in daycare and draw two big sticks holding a little stick with a happy face
between them. They come over to my place,
Sally sits on Dad's lap and sucks her thumb,
hungrily or sadly, we ask which one?
She doesn't know the words for what she feels
yet, so she shrugs her answer: *Don't worry,*
I'm okay. We play Alphabet. Greg says,
A, and I answer, *Apple.* Sally laughs,
unstoppering her mouth. We have a ways
before we get to the letter for *love.*

Meditations with Hildegard of Bingen (excerpt)
Hildegard of Bingen

Now in the people
that were meant to green,
there is no more life of any kind.
There is only shrivelled barrenness.

The winds are burdened
by the utterly awful stink of evil,
selfish goings-on.

Thunderstorms menace.
The air belches out
the filthy uncleanliness of the peoples.

There pours forth an unnatural,
a loathsome darkness,
that withers the green,
and wizens the fruit
that was to serve as food for the people.

Sometimes this layer of air
is full,
full of a fog that is the source
of many destructive and barren creatures,
that destroy and damage the earth,
rendering it incapable
of sustaining humanity.

The Journey (excerpt)
Lillian Smith

Without words, it comes. And suddenly, sharply, one is aware of being separated from every person on one's earth and every object, and from the beginning of things and from the future and even a little, from one's self. A moment before one was happily playing; the world was round and friendly. Now at one's feet there are chasms that had been invisible until this moment. And one knows, and never remembers how it was learned, that there will always be chasms, and across the chasms will always be those one loves.

Solstice Poem (excerpt)
Margaret Atwood

In this house (in a dying orchard,
behind it a tributary
of the wilderness, in front a road),
my daughter dances
unsteadily with a knitted bear.

Her father, onetime soldier,
touches my arm.
Worn language clots our throats,
making it difficult to say
what we mean, making it
difficult to see.

Instead we sing in the back room, raising
our pagan altar
of oranges and silver flowers:
our fools' picnic, our signal,
our flame, our nest, our fragile golden
protest against murder.

Outside, the cries of the birds
are rumours we hear clearly
but can't yet understand. Fresh ice
glints on the branches.

          In this dark
space of the year, the earth
turns again toward the sun, or

we would like to hope so.

Moving
Jeanne Foster

Each morning and each noon
and each late afternoon, and times
in between, I am stopping beside my old building
to observe patiently

my flowers. My geraniums
of three colors—the brightest pink
Bill started from a stick; and my variegated
sweet William, planted to blossom
the next, lost, time our two lives
came together; and the California poppy,
which migrated from Alice's plot
around the corner—Alice who is no longer
here; and the tender, green shoots
of dahlias, pushing through the dirt
at the base of last year's dried stalks
and being nipped as they do
by some secret thief of the dark. I am stopping
each day to look with dry eyes
and pray for another life. The lavender-veined
amaryllis is over and done with;
the gladiolus have yet to begin
their blossoming and their leaning. The cosmos
have come up all over,
small, feathery trees. Every now and then,
I kneel to flick away a weed
or to look more closely. Other times
I stand back like a proud hen.
And then I get angry, because the airlines
are on strike and Bill can't get a flight
in; because our President is standing tall,
and the right Reverend is on his
right hand. Because a retired Army man
rammed the Sacramento abortion clinic
with a World War II, amphibious "duck"; and my luck
is bad of late. Because Jim Luguri died
of a heart attack at thirty-nine; and
it isn't fair. Because things heal
in the sunshine. And Jim Wright
died too. And my little life
will go on. And I am never thankful
enough. And I can't stay
in this place. And the begonias have thickened,
finally, into a border. And the snap dragons
are yellow. And it is important to keep
watching and to keep growing. I am
filling my eyes with my flowers
and asking, Who will care for them
when I'm gone?
Who will care?

Misguided
Harriet Brown

I knew he would speak to me
before he did, asking directions,
holding the map out as if it, too,
were a question. We stood side by side
as the train raced under the river,
under that sudden weight. His breath
was licorice and root, was China
and the cramped, chilly room
he lived in now. He brought out
paper, wrote in a careful hand
his name, a number. I don't remember
the exact moment of offering,
of acceptance, but walking home
I found his name clutched in my hand
as if I were the one who could be saved.
He must have known I would not call.
It must have been a sudden lapse of generosity
that made me take what I could not return.
The moon was bright and everything
along the street seemed absolutely lucid
through its sheen of memory and loss,
of homesickness. I tore the paper
into bits and let them fall behind me,
casually, so that anyone watching
could not know how much they meant.

Christmas Letter, 1970 (excerpt)
May Sarton

"Yes," you say, "of course at Christmas
Half the world is suicidal."
And you are there. You answer the phone—
The wry voice with laughter in it.
Again and again the lifeline is thrown out.
There is no end to the work of salvage
In the drowning high seas of Christmas
When loneliness, in the name of Christ
(That longing!), attacks the world.

Town I Left

Helen Sorrells

In that town were hard spaces
of no trees growing, a sky
I wore on my head like a tin
wash basin, noon
a bleaching wind,
the land bleached
and I, too, lost all color.

Some say the young look on death
quickly and then away. Perhaps.
I only know in that town
I was young and I looked full
in death's stiffening face,
I heard its voice
selling shoes and rice and bricks,
I heard it in chains of porch swings
rusting the winter winds,
its cough from crows
in the cottonwoods,
among people sucked too dry
by their own all-day dying
to care about mine.

S M

Alice Walker

I tell you, Chickadee
I am afraid of people
who cannot cry
Tears left unshed
turn to poison
in the ducts
Ask the next soldier you see
enjoying a massacre
if this is not so.

People who do not cry
are victims
of soul mutilation
paid for in Marlboros
and trucks.

Resist.

Violence does not work
except for the man
who pays your salary
Who knows
if you could still weep
you would not take the job.

My Mother, Who Came from China, Where She Never Saw Snow

Laureen Mar

In the huge, rectangular room, the ceiling
a machinery of pipes and fluorescent lights,
ten rows of women hunch over machines,
their knees pressing against pedals
and hands pushing the shiny fabric thick as tongues
through metal and thread.
My mother bends her head to one of these machines.
Her hair is coarse and wiry, black as burnt scrub.
She wears glasses to shield her intense eyes.
A cone of orange thread spins. Around her,
talk flutters harshly in Toisan wah.
Chemical stings. She pushes cloth
through a pounding needle, under, around, and out,
breaks thread with a snap against fingerbone, tooth.
Sleeve after sleeve, sleeve.
It is easy. The same piece.
For eight or nine hours, sixteen bundles maybe,
250 sleeves to ski coats, all the same.
It is easy, only once she's run the needle
through her hand. She earns money
by each piece, on a good day,

thirty dollars. Twenty-four years.
It is frightening how fast she works.
She and the women who were taught sewing
terms in English as Second Language.
Dull thunder passes through their fingers.

Lady on a Bus
Jeanne Lohmann

Somebody treat her real bad.

Easy to see how it was when she
come down the middle of the bus,
big lady in tired old clothes,
brown silk dress hangin loose,
shufflin them dirty pink slippers.

Back of the bus ain't nowhere
for a strong black woman. Front
ain't noplace neither. So she
keep movin round, loud talkin
all the time, mad at everybody.

She had this whingding goin and she
didn't stop once, scarin them poor
white ladies. She was a snake charmer
they watched out the sides of they eyes,
lips goin tight, mouths gettin little.

Made one old lady move, called her bitch.
She jus kep firin away, badmouthin
the first Chinese she saw, yellin at her,
"Who better lookin anyway?" They was
all trapped and scared by that big Mama.

Her steam keep comin out, hot all over.
They clucked soft like chickens while
she cover that bus like a stormcloud.
People huggin them seats mighty close.
Nowhere to go. Nobody sayin nothin.

But if looks coulda done it, that woman
woulda been long gone. Her with her queen's face,
her eyes huntin someplace to rest, strong hands
movin up and down on the good bones in her head.

Everybody watchin and tryin not to.
Everybody part of what's wrong.

Somebody treat her real bad.

I Check My Parents' House
Julia Alvarez

I check my parents' house while they're abroad
during a weekend in New York. I drive
through their exclusive neighborhood, arrive
at dusk, remembering Mother's horror
stories of recent break-ins within blocks.
The door's rigged up with an alarm, three locks,
and inside, an emergency button,
which if I press will make the police come.
The windows are all wired to the alarm
and can't be opened. Despite this, five times
they've gotten in and robbed them clean. Inside
the key box in the hall, I find a sealed
envelope: FOR OUR FOUR DAUGHTERS, OPEN
ONLY IN CASE OF DEATH FOR INSTRUCTIONS.

The History of My Feeling
Kathleen Fraser

for D.

The history of my feeling for you (or is it the way you
   change
and are blameless like clouds)
                     reminds me of the sky in Portland

and the morning I unpacked
and found the white plates from Iowa City
broken,
      consistently surprising with cracks,
petals like new math theories smashed
          with the purposeful fingers of chance.
I loved the plates. They were remnants from an auction
which still goes on in my head because of the auc-
   tioneer's body
and his sexy insinuations about the goods he was selling.

But to Ruth, who talked them into their thin wraps of
   newspaper,
what we were sharing was departure and two lives
   breaking
and learning
       to mend into new forms.

We had loved our husbands,
         torn our bodies in classic ways to bear
           children: Sammy, David, Wesley—
Now we loved new men and wept together
so that the plates weren't important and hadn't been
   packed
with the care I might have given had I been alone.
But Ruth was with me.
You were gone, like the storm that's been arriving and
   disappearing
all morning.

      I awoke to hear heavy rain in the gutters.
The light was uncertain and my feelings had grown less
   sure.
Last night, pinned by a shaft of pain—
        your presence and your absence—
I knew clearly that I hated you
for entering me profoundly, for taking me inside you,
for husbanding me, claiming all that I knew
          and did not know,
yet letting me go from you
into this unpredictable and loneliest of weathers.

Hand games
Marge Piercy

Intent gets blocked by noise.
How often what we spoke
in the bathtub, weeping
water to water, what we framed
lying flat in bed to the spiked
night is not the letter that arrives,
the letter we thought we sent. We drive
toward each other on expressways
without exits. The telephone
turns our voices into codes,
then decodes the words falsely,
terms of an equation
that never balances, a scale
forever awry with its foot
stuck up lamely like a scream.

Drinking red wine from a sieve,
trying to catch love in words,
its strong brown river in flood
pours through our weak bones.
A kitten will chase the beam of a flash
light over the floor. We learn
some precious and powerful forces
cannot be touched, and what
we touch plump and sweet
as a peach from the tree, a tomato
from the vine, sheds the name
as if we tried to write in pencil
on its warm and fragrant skin.

Mostly the television is on
and the washer is running and the kettle
shrieks it's boiling while the telephone
rings. Mostly we are worrying about
the fuel bill and how to pay the taxes
and whether the diet is working
when the moment of vulnerability
lights on the nose like a blue moth,
then flitters away. In the leaking
sieve of our bodies we carry
the blood of our love.

The friend
Marge Piercy

We sat across the table.
he said, cut off your hands.
they are always poking at things.
they might touch me.
I said yes.

Food grew cold on the table.
he said, burn your body.
it is not clean and smells like sex.
it rubs my mind sore.
I said yes.

I love you, I said.
that's very nice, he said
I like to be loved,
that makes me happy.
Have you cut off your hands yet?

Housewife
Susan Fromberg Schaeffer

What can be wrong
That some days I hug this house
About me like a shawl, and feel
Each window like a tatter in its skin,
Or worse, bright eyes I must not look through?

Now my husband stands above me
As high as ever my father did
And I am in that house of dolls, which,
When young I could not shrink to.

I feel the shrinkage in each bone.
No matter what I do, my two girls
Spoil like fruit. Already they push us back
Like too-full plates. They play with us
Like dolls.

The road before the house is like a wish
That stretches out and out and will not
Stop, and the smallest hills are built
Like steps to the slippery moon,
But I
Circle this lit house like any moth
And see each day open its fingers
To disclose the stone—which hand?
Which hand? and the stone in both.

Once, I drove my car into a tree.
The bottles in the back
Burst like bombs, tubular glass beasts,
Giving up the ghost. My husband
Thought it was the road. It was.
In the rear-view mirror, it curved and curled,
Longer and stronger than the road ahead,
A question of perspective, I thought then.
I watched it til it turned, and I did not.
I breathed in pain like air,
As if, I, the rib, had cracked.

I did not feel this pain, not then,
Almost in my mouth. I wiggle this life
And find it loose. Like my girls,
I would pull it out, would watch
Something new and white
Push like mushrooms from the rich red soil.
But there is just this hole, this bone.

So I live inside my wedding ring,
Inside its arch,
Multiplying the tables of my days,
Rehearsing the lessons of this dish, that sleeve,
Wanting the book that no one wrote,
Loving my husband, my children, my house
With this pain in my jaw,
Wanting to go.

Do others feel like this? Where do they go?

Homes of Single Women (excerpt)
Susan B. Anthony

If women will not accept marriage *with subjection*, nor men proffer it *without*, there is, there can be, *no alternative*. The women who will *not be ruled* must live without marriage. And during this transition period, wherever, for the main-tenance of self-respect on the one side, and education into recognition of equality on the other, single women make comfortable and attractive homes for themselves, they furnish the best and most efficient object lessons for men.

The Second Sex (excerpt)
Simone de Beauvoir

Men have vied with one another in proclaiming that love is a woman's supreme accomplishment. "A woman who loves as a woman becomes only the more feminine," says Nietzsche; and Balzac: "Among the first-rate, man's life is fame, woman's life is love. Woman is man's equal only when she makes her life a perpetual offering, as that of man is perpetual action." But therein, again, is a cruel deception, since what she offers, men are in no wise anxious to accept. Man has no need of the unconditional devotion he claims, nor of the idola-trous love that flatters his vanity; he accepts them only on condition that he need not satisfy the reciprocal demands these attitudes imply. He preaches to woman that she should give—and her gifts bore him to distraction; she is left in embarrassment with her useless offerings, her empty life. On the day when it will be possible for woman to love not in her weakness but in her strength, not to escape herself but to find herself, not to abase herself but to assert her-self—on that day love will become for her, as for man, a source of life and not of mortal danger.

Conversation with a Fireman from Brooklyn
Tess Gallagher

> He offers, between planes,
> to buy me a drink. I've never talked
> to a fireman before, not one from Brooklyn
> anyway. Okay. Fine, I say. Somehow

the subject is bound to come up, women
firefighters, and since I'm
a woman and he's a fireman, between
the two of us, we know something
about this subject. Already
he's telling me he doesn't mind
women firefighters, but what
they look like
after fighting a fire, well
they lose all respect. He's sorry, but
he looks at them
covered with the cinders of someone's
lost hope, and he feels disgust, he just
wants to turn the hose on them, they
are that sweaty and stinking, just like
him, of course, but not the woman he
wants, you get me? and to come to that—
isn't it too bad, to be despised
for what you do to prove yourself
among men
who want to love you, to love you,
love you.

Clearing the Air
Nancy Willard

It's been ten years since you tried to kill me.
Biking home one night, I saw only your legs
stepping behind a tree, then you fell on my throat
like a cat. My books crashed the birds out of sleep.
We rolled in the leaves like lovers. My eyes popped
like Christmas lights, veins snapped, your teeth wore

my blood, your fingers left bars on my neck.
I can't remember your name,
and I saw your face only in court.
You sat in a box, docile as old shoes.
And I, who had never felt any man's weight
sometimes felt yours for nights afterwards.

Well, I'm ready to forgive
and I don't want to forget.
Sometimes I tell myself that we met
differently, on a train. You give me
a Batman comic and show me your passport.
I have nothing but my report card.

but I offer my mother's fudge for the grapes
rotting the one paper bag you carry.
In my tale you are younger and loved.
Outside you live in a thousand faces
and so do your judges, napping in parks,
rushing to fires, folded like bats on the truck,

mad and nude in a white Rolls
pinching dollars and leather behinds.
Burned from a tree by your betters, you take
to the streets and hang in the dark like a star,
making me see your side, waking me
with the blows and the weight of it.

Farmwife
Betsy Sholl

The woman who has nodded to me from her porch
for weeks, still nods now, bobs her head
leading me inside to see
21 grandchildren posed on a shelf,
sills full of colored glass.

Twice, I heard, she left her husband
and then returned.

He stays outside with the dogs,
hollering them away from the barn.

Chickens flutter and squall,
leaving patches of brown feathers.

She says she's been nodding 26 years.
The doctor calls it "the trembles,"
but she knows something sharper
is pecking her brain.

Twice his fists have hit,
knocked her against the wall.
Twice she's returned

to faces of grandchildren
perfectly still in the tilt
of their frames, glass
shining on every sill,

to hens squawking themselves into trees
whenever a dog comes near:
She sweeps up the puddles
of brown and white feathers
that fear sends flying,

pours them into ticking
to cushion her relentless,
affirming head.

The Victim

Ellen Bryant Voigt

Who could remember cause? Both
sought injury, and God knows
they were perfectly matched for pain.
Fenced into their landscape of passion,
each moved to the center and set upon
the other. Always, she would deploy
the tease, the jab, the deft tongue,
until his arm swung out on its hinge,
coming flat-handed against her face,
recoiled, then stiffened to thrust
his fist into her open mouth.
This was not the only violation.
When a child is struck by her father,
she crawls toward him, not away,
bound by habits not yet broken.

Killers of the Dream (excerpt)
Lillian Smith

Something was wrong with a world that tells you that love is good and people are important and then forces you to deny love and to humiliate people. I knew, though I would not for years confess it aloud, that in trying to shut the Negro race away from us, we have shut ourselves away from so many good, creative, honest, deeply human things in life. I began to understand slowly at first but more clearly as the years passed, that the warped, distorted frame we have put around every Negro child from birth is around every white child also. Each is on a different side of the frame but each is pinioned there. And I knew that what cruelly shapes and cripples the personality of one is as cruelly shaping and crippling the personality of the other. I began to see that though we may, as we acquire new knowledge, live through new experiences, examine old memories, gain the strength to tear the frame from us, yet we are stunted and warped and in our lifetime cannot grow straight again any more than can a tree, put in a steel-like twisting frame when young, grow tall and straight when the frame is torn away at maturity.

Adulthood
Nikki Giovanni

(for claudia)

i usta wonder who i'd be

when i was a little girl in indianapolis
sitting on doctors porches with post-dawn pre-debs
(wondering would my aunt drag me to church sunday)
i was meaningless
and i wondered if life
would give me a chance to mean

i found a new life in the withdrawal from all things
not like my image

when i was a teen-ager i usta sit
on front steps conversing
the gym teachers son with embryonic eyes
about the essential essence of the universe

(and other bullshit stuff)
recognizing the basic powerlessness of me

but then i went to college where i learned
that just because everything i was was unreal
i could be real and not just real through withdrawal
into emotional crosshairs or colored bourgeoisie intellectual pretensions
but from involvement with things approaching reality
i could possibly have a life

so catatonic emotions and time wasting sex games
were replaced with functioning commitments to logic and
necessity and the gray area was slowly darkened into
a black thing
for a while progress was being made along with a certain degree
of happiness cause i wrote a book and found a love
and organized a theatre and even gave some lectures on
Black history
and began to believe all good people could get
together and win without bloodshed
then
hammarskjold was killed
and lumumba was killed
and diem was killed
and kennedy was killed
and malcolm was killed
and evers was killed
and schwerner, chaney and goodman were killed
and liuzzo was killed
and stokely fled the country
and le roi was arrested
and rap was arrested
and pollard, thompson and cooper were killed
and king was killed
and kennedy was killed
and i sometimes wonder why i didn't become a debutante
sitting on porches, going to church all the time, wondering
is my eye make-up on straight
or a withdrawn discoursing on the stars and moon
instead of a for real Black person who must now feel
and inflict
pain

Watts (excerpt)
Shirley Kaufman

he's learning to shoot
with his children, teaching them how
with a gun, and last week
he hit the bull's eye at fifty feet
twenty times out of twenty.

The son who sings in the choir
wins prizes. The youngest, a girl,
plays the flute and the cello.
The middle one studies hard.

    Why?
I ask
wanting to start over.
    Why?

    We all need a gun
in the house. Learn
to use one. The first time
I fired it, they jumped.
    Now they love it. And Watts,
he says.
    Think about Watts.

Yom Kippur
Chana Bloch

Our new clothes fool no one.
A year of days. The fingernails
keep growing, even
in life.

We are tight for winter, brooding
in this vat of used air.
As if we could hatch
some glory out of our sitting here still.

What shrinks inside us, these stones
that rattle in our throats
tell us only
to go on getting older.

But the eyes want, the fingers, the emptiness
of the mouth
wants something to speak to, some lost
horn of a mouth with its unpredictable answers.

On the eastern wall, the lions
stand fast,
raising their braided heads,
their gold tongues whetted.

The Will toward the Good

Rarely do we see in the work of women poets the kind of despair and angst that is so common in contemporary male writing. Rather, there seems to be the assumption running through much of women's poetry that hope is real and change is indeed possible. How does change come? Through the sensitive and loving concern of persons, each for the other, and a willingness to do the hard work of organizing and planning in order to change society. We must witness by voice and by deed. In the selections that follow, the writers characteristically do not stand aloof from societal problems, but instead accept their own complicity in what is, and take the responsibility upon themselves to make a better world than we yet have made.

To a Milkweed

Deborah Digges

Teach me to love what I've made, and judgment
in that love.

Teach me your arrogance.
With each five-petaled horned flower teach me

how much blossoming matters
                                    along roadsides, dry-

beds, these fields no longer cleared.
Teach me such patience at each turning, how

to live on nothing but will, its milky
juices, poison

to the others, though when its stem is broken,
bleeds. Teach me to

need the future,
                    and the past, that Indian summer.

Let me be tricked into believing
that by what moves in me I might be saved,

and hold to this. Hold
onto this until there's wind enough.

Memoirs, I (excerpt)

Margaret Fuller

In the chamber
of death, I prayed
in very early years,
"Give me truth;
cheat me by no illusion."
O, the granting of
this prayer is

sometimes terrible to me!
I walk over the
burning ploughshares,
and they sear
my feet. Yet nothing but
the truth will do.

To Softness

Laurie Sheck

Under junk heaps and stripped and burning cars
and bombed-out buildings,
under iron and tin and plastic,
under U.S. Steel and Coca-Cola
and the bridge repainted silver to cover all the black
graffitied hearts and birds and names,
beneath underpass and overpass,
under timetables, profitability, summits,
margins of error and cuts,
under for your own good and in our best interest,
under front-runner, leveraged buyouts, arms deals,
state of the union, and rates of exchange,
it must be there like an ash heap
but alive, like a veil, a half-formed thought
throbbing its slow pulse behind the lips,
a softness, a tenderness,
a hand turning pages throughout the night
in a bare room, eyes at the window,
breath at the door, something in need of protection,
something capable of feeling harm.

This Morning
Muriel Rukeyser

Waking this morning,
a violent woman in the violent day
laughing.
    Past the line of memory
along the long body of your life
in which move childhood, youth, your lifetime of touch,
eyes, lips, chest, belly, sex, legs, to the waves of the sheet.
I look past the little plant
on the city windowsill
to the tall towers bookshapes, crushed together in greed,
the river flashing flowing corroded,
the intricate harbor and the sea, the wars, the moon the planets
      all who people space
in the sun visible invisible.
African violets in the light
breathing, in a breathing universe. I want strong peace, and delight,
the wild good.
I want to make my touch poems:
to find my morning, to find you entire
alive moving among the anti-touch people.

    I say across the waves of the air to you:
today once more
I will try to be non-violent
one more day
this morning, waking the world away
in the violent day

The Gardener
Robin Becker

She works and works against sadness
stilling grief with a spade.
Only the dead have come
home to their faithful hungers
and in spring, when they speak, she opens
the ground and puts in something

green the dead can climb. Small pine
and spruce in their poor burlap.
Lilacs. Dogwood.
                    She thinks of catkins
softening the air and of the lost
dog who listened with his nose.
She leans against his body the weight of her love
and walks through a forest
dim behind cataracts but luminous in a memory
her grandmother conjured tree by tree.
She cuts back the grape vines and clears
the roses, taking the curse
out of the stiff ground.

The Woman with the Wild-Grown Hair Relaxes after Another Long Day
Nita Penfold

After she drives her younger daughter to school, struggling
to get the wheelchair out without running over her foot and
the car stalls for the fifth time as she leaves because of
the cracked distributor cap;

after she meets the new cashier's stare over her food stamps
at the Star Market going to buy soda crackers and soup and
gingerale for another daughter who is home sick after
throwing up her entire dinner in the middle of the night;

after she exchanges babysitting for their rent in the main house
downstairs with the sweet fat/baby and blonde sister who owns
nine Little Ponies in their pink castle and a Pig-Faced Doll
with its very own brass bed;

after she lugs out the deep steel pot to catch the rain dripping
from the skylight and kills the horde of fungus/gnats in the
bathroom with their thin wings splayed against the white walls
like Christmas miniatures of squashed angels;

after she spends an hour with the child psychologist explaining
why she thinks her marriage failed and how it has affected
the children's lives and she wonders aloud if she can take
much more of this and still be able to write poems;

after the dishes, the laundry, the second daughter's throwing-up,
after trying to scrub the permanent ring out of the clawfoot tub
and fixing the cabinet door so it won't scrape the wall when
it opens;

after all of this, she soaks in bubbled bathwater and thinks of
Job's unnamed wife, caught between a righteous husband and his
war between God and Satan—how that woman must have tried to
smother the heavenly fire with her mantle as it destroyed their
sheep and servants, and—fiercely—dug at the stones that killed
her ten children when the great wind breathed from the wilderness
to topple their home; how she tended Job's sores, washing him
gently with cool water, soothing the flame of Satan's tongue,
comforting him, and how she stood alone while he debated his
faith with God, proved himself again worthy to give this wife
another ten children to raise.

As she rubs her tight thighs with a worn washcloth, she thinks
about the faith of women creating foundations out of their flesh,
becoming the anonymous survivors of daily battles,
that never seem to win the war.

When he came (excerpt)
Dorothee Sölle

He needs you
that's all there is to it
without you he's left hanging
goes up in dachau's smoke
is sugar and spice in the baker's hands
gets revalued in the next stock market crash
he's consumed and blown away
used up
without you

Help him
that's what faith is
he can't bring it about
his kingdom
couldn't then couldn't later can't now
not at any rate without you
and that is his irresistible appeal

Prayer for a Tenspeed Heart
Barbara Hendryson

Let the fire of my body
propel and warm me
and let each darkness
reveal its plenitude.

Let the hills
flatten under my wheels
and let the eloquent curves
yield up their good surprise.

Let my heart be obstinate
when I need to climb
and let my lowliest gears
restrain my spinning down.

Let there be flatland, too,
and into that glittering place
let me stretch with the heart of a lover,
at full speed, blind and intent.

Aunt Jane of Kentucky (excerpt)
Eliza Calvert Hall

"I've had a heap o' comfort all my life makin' quilts, and now in my old age I wouldn't take a fortune for 'em. . . . You see, some folks has albums to put folks' pictures in to remember 'em by, and some folks has a book and writes down the things that happen every day so they won't forgit 'em; but, honey, these quilts is my albums and my di'ries, and whenever the weather's bad and I can't git out to see folks, I jest spread out my quilts and look at 'em and study over 'em, and it's jest like goin' back fifty or sixty years and livin' my life over again. . . .

*

"Did you ever think, child, . . . how much piecin' a quilt's like livin' a life? And as for sermons, why, they ain't no better sermon to me than a patchwork quilt, and the doctrines is right there a heap plainer'n they are in the catechism. Many a time I've set and listened to Parson Page preachin' about predestination and free-will, and I've said to myself, 'Well, I ain't never been through Centre College up at Danville, but if I could jest git up in the pulpit with one of my quilts, I could make it a heap plainer to folks than parson's makin' it with all his big words.' You see, you start out with jest so much caliker; you don't go to the store and pick it out and buy it, but the neighbors will give you a piece here and a piece there, and you'll have a piece left every time you cut out a dress, and you take jest what happens to come. And that's like predestination. But when it comes to the cuttin' out, why, you're free to choose your own pattern. You can give the same kind o' pieces to two persons, and one'll make a 'nine-patch' and one'll make a 'wild-goose chase,' and there'll be two quilts made out o' the same kind o' pieces, and jest as different as they can be. And that is jest the way with livin'. The Lord sends us the pieces, but we can cut 'em out and put 'em together pretty much to suit ourselves, and there's a heap more in the cuttin' out and the sewin' than there is in the caliker. . . .

*

"I've been a hard worker all my life, . . . but 'most all my work has been the kind that 'perishes with the usin',' as the Bible says. That's the discouragin' thing about a woman's work. Milly Amos used to say that if a woman was to see all the dishes that she had to wash before she died, piled up before her in one pile, she'd lie down and die right then and there. . . . But when one o' my grandchildren or great-grandchildren sees one o' these quilts, they'll think about Aunt Jane, and, wherever I am then, I'll know I ain't forgotten.

"I reckon everybody wants to leave somethin' behind that'll last after they're dead and gone. It don't look like it's worth while to live unless you can do that. . . . Now, some folks has money to build monuments with—great, tall, marble pillars, with angels on top of 'em, like you see in Cave Hill and them big city curyin'-grounds. And some folks can build churches and schools and hospitals to keep folks in mind of 'em, but all the work I've got to leave behind me is jest these quilts, and sometimes, when I'm settin' here, workin' with my caliker and gingham pieces, I'll finish off a block, and I laugh and say to myself, 'Well, here's another stone for the monument.' "

The Oven Loves the TV Set

Heather McHugh

Stuck on the fridge, our favorite pin-up girl
is anorexic. On the radio we have a riff

of Muzak sax, and on the mind
a self-help book. We sprawl all evening, all

alone, in an unraised ranch;
all day the company we kept

kept on incorporating. As for worlds
of poverty, we do our best, thanks

to a fund of Christian feeling
and mementos from

Amelia, the foster child, who has
the rags and seven photogenic sisters we require

in someone to be saved. She's proof
Americans have got a heart

to go with all that happy
acumen you read about. We love

a million little prettinesses,
decency, and ribbons on

the cockapoo. But who
will study alphabets for hands? Who gives

a damn what goes into
a good wheelchair? Who lugs the rice

from its umpteen stores
to the ends of the earth, to even one

dead-end? Not we.
Our constitutional pursuit

is happiness, i.e.
somebody nice, and not

too fat, we can have
for our personal friend.

3 : 6 (excerpt)
Alta

one hesitates to bring a child into this world without fixing
it up a little. paint a special room. stop sexism. learn how
to love. vow to do it better than it was done when you were
a baby. vow to make, if necessary, *new* mistakes. vow to be
awake for the birth. to believe in joy even in the midst of
unbearable pain.

A Few Sirens
Alice Walker

Today I am at home
writing poems.
My life goes well:
only a few sirens herald disaster
in the ghetto
down the street.
In the world, people die
of hunger.
On my block we lose
jobs, housing and breasts.
But in the world
children are lost;
whole countries of children
starved to death
before the age
of five
each year;

their mothers squatted
in the filth
around the empty cooking pot
wondering:

But I cannot pretend
to know
what they wonder.
A walled horror
instead of thought
would be my mind.

And our children
gladly starve themselves.

Thinking of the food I eat
every day
I want to vomit, like
people who throw up
at will,
understanding that whether
they digest or not
they must consume.

Can you imagine?

Rather than let the hungry
inside the restaurants
Let them eat vomit, they say.
They are applauded
for this.
They are light.

But
wasn't there a time
when food was sacred?

When a dead child
starved naked
among the oranges
in the marketplace
spoiled
the appetite?

The Network of the Imaginary Mother (excerpt)
Robin Morgan

Blessed be my brain
    that I may conceive of my own power.
Blessed be my breast
    that I may give sustenance to those I love.
Blessed be my womb
    that I may create what I choose to create.
Blessed be my knees
    that I may bend so as not to break.
Blessed be my feet
    that I may walk in the path of my highest will.

Mother's Day Proclamation of 1870
Julia Ward Howe

Arise, then women of this day!
Arise all women who have hearts,
Whether your baptism be that of water or of tears!
Say firmly:
"We will not have questions decided by irrelevant agencies,
Our husbands shall not come to us, reeking of carnage,
for caresses and applause.
Our sons shall not be taken from us to unlearn
all that we have been able to teach them of charity, mercy and patience.
We women of one country
will be too tender of those of another country
to allow our sons to be trained to injure theirs."
From the bosom of the devastated earth a voice goes up with
our own, it says 'disarm, disarm!'
The sword of murder is not the balance of justice.
Blood does not wipe out dishonor
Nor violence indicate possession.
As men have often forsaken the plow and the anvil at the summons of war,
Let women now leave all that may be left of home
For a great and earnest day of counsel.
Let them meet first, as women, to bewail and commemorate the dead.
Let them then solemnly take counsel with each other as to the means

whereby the great human family can live in peace,
each bearing after his own time the sacred impress, not of Caesar,
But of God.
In the name of womanhood and humanity, I earnestly ask
that a general congress of women without limit of nationality,
be appointed and held at some place deemed most convenient
and at the earliest period consistent with its objects,
to promote the alliance of the different nationalities,
the amicable settlement of international questions,
the great and general interests of peace.

The low road

Marge Piercy

What can they do
to you? Whatever they want.
They can set you up, they can
bust you, they can break
your fingers, they can
burn your brain with electricity,
blur you with drugs till you
can't walk, can't remember, they can
take your child, wall up
your lover. They can do anything
you can't stop them
from doing. How can you stop
them? Alone, you can fight,
you can refuse, you can
take what revenge you can
but they roll over you.

But two people fighting
back to back can cut through
a mob, a snake-dancing file
can break a cordon, an army
can meet an army.

Two people can keep each other
sane, can give support, conviction,
love, massage, hope, sex.
Three people are a delegation,

a committee, a wedge. With four
you can play bridge and start
an organization. With six
you can rent a whole house,
eat pie for dinner with no
seconds, and hold a fund raising party.
A dozen make a demonstration.
A hundred fill a hall.
A thousand have solidarity and your own newsletter;
ten thousand, power and your own paper;
a hundred thousand, your own media;
ten million, your own country.

It goes on one at a time,
it starts when you care
to act, it starts when you do
it again after they said no,
it starts when you say *We*
and know who you mean, and each
day you mean one more.

The seven of pentacles
Marge Piercy

Under a sky the color of pea soup
she is looking at her work growing away there
actively, thickly like grapevines or pole beans
as things grow in the real world, slowly enough.
If you tend them properly, if you mulch, if you water,
if you provide birds that eat insects a home and winter food,
if the sun shines and you pick off caterpillars,
if the praying mantis comes and the ladybugs and the bees,
then the plants flourish, but at their own internal clock.

Connections are made slowly, sometimes they grow underground.
You cannot tell always by looking what is happening.
More than half a tree is spread out in the soil under your feet.
Penetrate quietly as the earthworm that blows no trumpet.
Fight persistently as the creeper that brings down the tree.
Spread like the squash plant that overruns the garden.
Gnaw in the dark and use the sun to make sugar.

Weave real connections, create real nodes, build real houses.
Live a life you can endure: make love that is loving.
Keep tangling and interweaving and taking more in,
a thicket and bramble wilderness to the outside but to us
interconnected with rabbit runs and burrows and lairs.

Live as if you liked yourself, and it may happen:
reach out, keep reaching out, keep bringing in.
This is how we are going to live for a long time: not always,
for every gardener knows that after the digging, after
   the planting,
after the long season of tending and growth, the harvest comes.

To be of use
Marge Piercy

The people I love the best
jump into work head first
without dallying in the shallows
and swim off with sure strokes almost out of sight.
They seem to become natives of that element,
the black sleek heads of seals
bouncing like half-submerged balls.

I love people who harness themselves, an ox to a heavy cart,
who pull like water buffalo, with massive patience,
who strain in the mud and the muck to move things forward,
who do what has to be done, again and again.

I want to be with people who submerge
in the task, who go into the fields to harvest
and work in a row and pass the bags along,
who stand in the line and haul in their places,
who are not parlor generals and field deserters
but move in a common rhythm
when the food must come in or the fire be put out.

The work of the world is common as mud.
Botched, it smears the hands, crumbles to dust.
But the thing worth doing well done
has a shape that satisfies, clean and evident.

Greek amphoras for wine or oil,
Hopi vases that held corn, are put in museums
but you know they were made to be used.
The pitcher cries for water to carry
and a person for work that is real.

A just anger
Marge Piercy

Anger shines through me.
Anger shines through me.
I am a burning bush.
My rage is a cloud of flame.
My rage is a cloud of flame
in which I walk
seeking justice
like a precipice.
How the streets
of the iron city
flicker, flicker,
and the dirty air
fumes.
Anger storms
between me and things,
transfiguring,
transfiguring.
A good anger acted upon
is beautiful as lightning
and swift with power.
A good anger swallowed,
a good anger swallowed
clots the blood
to slime.

It Is Dangerous to Read Newspapers

Margaret Atwood

While I was building neat
castles in the sandbox,
the hasty pits were
filling with bulldozed corpses

and as I walked to the school
washed and combed, my feet
stepping on the cracks in the cement
detonated red bombs.

Now I am grownup
and literate, and I sit in my chair
as quietly as a fuse

and the jungles are flaming, the under-
brush is charged with soldiers,
the names on the difficult
maps go up in smoke.

I am the cause, I am a stockpile of chemical
toys, my body
is a deadly gadget,
I reach out in love, my hands are guns,
my good intentions are completely lethal.

Even my
passive eyes transmute
everything I look at to the pocked
black and white of a war photo,
how
can I stop myself

Small Comfort
Katha Pollitt

Coffee and cigarettes in a clean café,
forsythia lit like a damp match against
a thundery sky drunk on its own ozone,

the laundry cool and crisp and folded away
again in the lavender closet—too late to find
comfort enough in such small daily moments

of beauty, renewal, calm, too late to imagine
people would rather be happy than suffering
and inflicting suffering. We're near the end,

but oh, before the end, as the sparrows wing
each night to their secret nests in the elm's green dome,
oh, let the last bus bring

lover to lover, let the starveling
dog turn the corner and lope suddenly,
miraculously, down its own street, home.

Holy the Firm (excerpt)
Annie Dillard

. . . Who shall ascend into the hill of the Lord? or who shall stand in his holy place? There is no one but us. There is no one to send, nor a clean hand, nor a pure heart on the face of the earth, nor in the earth, but only us, a generation comforting ourselves with the notion that we have come at an awkward time, that our innocent fathers are all dead—as if innocence had ever been—and our children busy and troubled, and we ourselves unfit, not yet ready, having each of us chosen wrongly, made a false start, failed, yielded to impulse and the tangled comfort of pleasures, and grown exhausted, unable to seek the thread, weak, and involved. But there is no one but us. There never has been.

Pilgrim at Tinker Creek (excerpt)
Annie Dillard

The secret of seeing is, then, the pearl of great price. If I thought he could teach me to find it and keep it forever I would stagger barefoot across a hundred deserts after any lunatic at all. But although the pearl may be found, it may not be sought. The literature of illumination reveals this above all: although it comes to those who wait for it, it is always, even to the most practiced and adept, a gift and a total surprise. I return from one walk knowing where the killdeer nests in the field by the creek and the hour the laurel blooms. I return from the same walk a day later scarcely knowing my own name. Litanies hum in my ears; my tongue flaps in my mouth Ailinon, alleluia! I cannot cause light; the most I can do is try to put myself in the path of its beam. It is possible, in deep space, to sail on solar wind. Light, be it particle or wave, has force: you rig a giant sail and go. The secret of seeing is to sail on solar wind. Hone and spread your spirit till you yourself are a sail, whetted, translucent, broadside to the merest puff.

Eagle Poem
Joy Harjo

To pray you open your whole self
To sky, to earth, to sun, to moon
To one whole voice that is you.
And know there is more
That you can't see, can't hear
Can't know except in moments
Steadily growing, and in languages
That aren't always sound but other
Circles of motion.
Like eagle that Sunday morning
Over Salt River. Circled in blue sky
In wind, swept our hearts clean
With sacred wings.
We see you, see ourselves and know
That we must take the utmost care
And kindness in all things.
Breathe in, knowing we are made of
All this, and breathe, knowing
We are truly blessed because we

Were born, and die soon, within a
True circle of motion,
Like eagle rounding out the morning
Inside us.
We pray that it will be done
In beauty.
In beauty.

The Day Before They Bombed Nagasaki

Rebecca Baggett

We sit at our kitchen table,
writing letters for the nuclear freeze.
Jars of applesauce stretch across the counter,
stained pink from the apple skins,
stores for the winter
that I do not trust we will have.

The after-light from Hiroshima and Nagasaki
has stained fifteen years of my life.
Every day a battle not to accept despair,
to pick the ripe apples before they fall,
to cook them, season them, pack them in jars
as if I were sure we would have a whole winter
to eat them, as if I were sure
there was a point in preserving something.
Every day a battle not to accept
the vision born of that light:
as I write, the skin across my fingers
tightens, strains back from my bones,
peels away like pink apple skin to bare
the crisp white bone beneath.

I pick the apples, store them for the winter
that I refuse to relinquish, the winter
in which I refuse despair.
I grip the black pen tighter,
and write as if my one thin sheet of paper
were a shield to lift between
Nagasaki and the light to come.

Gathered at the River
Denise Levertov

For Beatrice Hawley
and John Jagel

As if the trees were not indifferent . . .

A breeze flutters the candles but the trees give off
a sense of listening, of hush.

The dust of August on their leaves.
But it grows dark. Their dark green
is something known about, not seen.

But summer twilight takes away
only color, not form. The tree-forms,
massive trunks and the great domed heads,
leaning in towards us, are visible,

a half-circle of attention.

They listen because the war
we speak of, the human war with ourselves,

the war against earth,
against nature,
is a war against them.

The words are spoken
of those who survived a while,
living shadowgraphs, eyes fixed forever
on witnessed horror,
who survived to give
testimony, that no-one

may plead ignorance.
Contra naturam. The trees,
the trees are not indifferent.

We intone together, *Never again,*

we stand in a circle,
singing, speaking, making vows,

remembering the dead
of Hiroshima,
of Nagasaki.

We are holding candles: we kneel to set them
afloat on the dark river
as they do
there in Hiroshima. We are invoking

saints and prophets,
heroes and heroines of justice and peace,
to be with us, to help us
stop the torment of our evil dreams . . .

Windthreatened flames bob on the current . . .

They don't get far from shore. But none capsizes
even in the swell of a boat's wake.

The waxy paper cups sheltering them
catch fire. But still the candles
sail their gold downstream.

And still the trees ponder our strange doings, as if
well aware that if we fail,
we fail also for them:
if our resolves and prayers are weak and fail

there will be nothing left of their slow and innocent wisdom,

no roots,
no bole nor branch,

no memory
of shade,
of leaf,

no pollen.

Conspiracy
Claire Bateman

Why is it me they always sit beside
when rows of empty seats beg
for the reassurance of human weight?
I count the shirts he wears
while he tells me about NASA's secret plan
to inject everyone with drugs
that cancel the need for breath
in preparation for life underwater
or on the moon. His mission
is to warn the nation not to let them do it.
It's not God's plan for people to live
underwater or on the moon.
Tell your neighbors.
Warn your friends.
Resist while there's still time.

After he leaves, my breath nudges me
almost involuntarily, a delicate lover
that has haunted me since birth
like a family secret, a middle name, the Holy Ghost—
the first pleasure of surfacing,
the last souvenir to be given up to customs
on departure for some place
alien as the ocean,
airless as the moon.

Breath, I put my arms around you
and seal our pact with an impossible kiss.

Tell your neighbors.
Warn your friends.
Resist while there's still time.

Our Passion for Justice (excerpt)
Carter Heyward

Love, like truth and beauty, is concrete. Love is not fundamentally a sweet feeling; not, at heart, a matter of sentiment, attachment, or being "drawn toward." Love is active, effective, a matter of making reciprocal and mutually beneficial relation with one's friends and enemies. Love creates righteousness, or justice, here on earth. To make love is to make justice. As advocates and activists for justice know, loving involves struggle, resistance, risk. People working today on behalf of women, blacks, lesbians and gay men, the aging, the poor in this country and elsewhere know that making justice is not a warm, fuzzy experience. I think also that sexual lovers and good friends know that the most compelling relationships demand hard work, patience, and a willingness to endure tensions and anxiety in creating mutually empowering bonds.

For this reason loving involves *commitment*. We are not automatic lovers of self, others, world, or God. Love does not just happen. We are not love machines, puppets on the strings of a deity called "love." Love is a choice—not simply, or necessarily, a rational choice, but rather a willingness to be present to others without pretense or guile. Love is a conversion to humanity—a willingness to participate with others in the healing of a broken world and broken lives. Love is the choice to experience life as a member of the human family, a partner in the dance of life, rather than as an alien in the world or as a deity above the world, aloof and apart from human flesh.

Beginners
Denise Levertov

Dedicated to the memory of Karen Silkwood and Eliot Gralla

> 'From too much love of living,
> Hope and desire set free,
> Even the weariest river
> Winds somewhere to the sea—

> But we have only begun
> to love the earth.

> We have only begun
> to imagine the fulness of life.

How could we tire of hope?
—so much is in bud.

How can desire fail?
—we have only begun

to imagine justice and mercy,
only begun to envision

how it might be
to live as siblings with beast and flower,
not as oppressors.

Surely our river
cannot already be hastening
into the sea of nonbeing?

Surely it cannot
drag, in the silt,
all that is innocent?

Not yet, not yet—
there is too much broken
that must be mended,

too much hurt we have done to each other
that cannot yet be forgiven.

We have only begun to know
the power that is in us if we would join
our solitudes in the communion of struggle.

So much is unfolding that must
complete its gesture,

so much is in bud.

The Fountain

Denise Levertov

Don't say, don't say there is no water
to solace the dryness at our hearts.
I have seen

the fountain springing out of the rock wall
and you drinking there. And I too
before your eyes

found footholds and climbed
to drink the cool water.

The woman of that place, shading her eyes,
frowned as she watched—but not because
she grudged the water,

only because she was waiting
to see we drank our fill and were
refreshed.

Don't say, don't say there is no water.
That fountain is there among its scalloped
green and gray stones,

it is still there and always there
with its quiet song and strange power
to spring in us,
up and out through the rock.

Sacredness of the Ordinary

In women's writing there is little of the cultural dichotomy between the sacred and the profane. Again and again the writing suggests that we may profoundly experience the sacred in the ordinary tasks and pleasures of living, if we would but be open to these events as spirit-filled. Traditional religious themes are transformed in the light of down-to-earth human realities. Just what is marriage, anyway? And salvation? And the Virgin birth? The writers of the following pieces find blessings in putting a child to bed or in baking a loaf of fresh bread. They find the holy in steaming bathrooms, in wretched singers in church, in a bulb of garlic, or in an overweight couple shopping for condoms at the drugstore.

Matins (excerpt)
Denise Levertov

Marvelous Truth, confront us
at every turn,
in every guise, iron ball,
egg, dark horse, shadow,
cloud
of breath on the air,

dwell
in our crowded hearts
our steaming bathrooms, kitchens full of
things to be done, the
ordinary streets.

Thrust close your smile
that we know you, terrible joy.

The Acolyte
Denise Levertov

The large kitchen is almost dark.
Across the plain of even, diffused light,
copper pans on the wall and the window geranium
tend separate campfires.
Herbs dangle their Spanish moss from rafters.

At the table, floury hands
kneading dough, feet planted
steady on flagstones,
a woman ponders the loaves-to-be.
Yeast and flour, water and salt,
have met in the huge bowl.

It's not
the baked and cooled and cut
bread she's thinking of,
but the way
the dough rises and has a life of its own,

not the oven she's thinking of
but the way
the sour smell changes
to fragrance.

She wants to put
a silver rose or a bell of diamonds
into each loaf;
she wants

to bake a curse into one loaf,
into another, the words that break
evil spells and release
transformed heroes into their selves;
she wants to make
bread that is more than bread.

Moon of the First Communion
Kathleen Norris

for Lyndsay Rose Kane

For the girl, it was a growing up
to disillusion.
"Don't we get to do anything more?" she asked.
The moment had passed
and the wafer tasted like dry bread
that was gone too soon,
the wine tasted like wine.

Her eyes were troubled;
she took off her veil.
Later, she smiled
and graciously allowed her parents
their celebration,
picking out the fanciest ice cream cake
in the store, calling
her best friend Sarah
to come on over; and it was enough.

As for me,
the body of Christ, whatever it was,
was carried by the children
through the church
along with roses and potted plants
and self-portraits on newsprint
that they taped to the altar,
and the priest offered it
to anyone moved by God.

For the girl, more than anything,
I wanted to be part of it.
A woman handed me a wafer
that looked like the full moon,
another held a chalice of wine.
It tasted like sunlight
and warmed my throat a long time.

The Wedding in the Courthouse
Kathleen Norris

I don't like weddings.
When you live here
long enough
all the spindly legged girls
grow up like weeds
to be mowed down: matrons
at twenty-five, all edges taken off.
When the music starts
they're led down the aisle
in their white dresses
and we celebrate sentiment
and money.

There's only one wedding
I'd go to again.
I happened to be on an errand
at the county courthouse
and Lucille came running:
"Will you be a witness?
We need two,
and the girls can't leave their desks."

They'd shown up
that morning, no family or friends.
Not kids: he looked about thirty
and she just a little younger.
They couldn't stop smiling.
She might have been pregnant,
but you couldn't tell.
It might have been the denim jumper
she was wearing.

I can picture Lucille
chain-smoking: surprised
and pleased
to interrupt routine.
And the Deputy Sheriff,
a young man, blushing,
loaded gun in his holster,
arms hanging loose:
he looked at his shoes.
But it's the words
I remember most. It was as if
I was hearing them
for the first time.
Lucille put out a cigarette
and began: "Dearly beloved,"
and we were!

The Sky Is Full of Blue and Full of the Mind of God

Kathleen Norris

for Odo Muggli, O.S.B.

A girl wrote that once
for me, in winter, in a school
at Minot Air Force Base.
A girl tall for her age,
with cornrows and a shy, gap-toothed smile.
She was lonely in North Dakota,

I think: for God, for trees,
warm weather, the soft cadences of Louisiana.
I think of her as the sky stretches tight
all around.

I'm at the Conoco on I-94, waiting for the eastbound bus.
Mass is not over: the towers of the monastery
give no sign that, deep in the church,
men in robes and chasubles
are playing at a serious game.

I feel like dancing on this
wooden porch: "Gotta get to you, baby,
been runnin' all over town."
The jukebox is wired to be heard outside
and I dance to keep warm,
my breath carried white on the breeze.

The sky stretches tight, a mandorla of cloud
around the sun. And now
Roy Orbison reaches for the stratosphere:
something about a blue angel.
It is the Sanctus; I know it; I'm ready.

"Scientists find universe awash in tiny diamonds"*
Pat Mayne Ellis

But haven't we always known?
The shimmer of trees, the shaking of flames
every cloud lined with something
clean water sings
right to the belly
scouring us with its purity
it too is awash with diamonds

"so small that trillions could rest
on the head of a pin"

*quotations found in a newspaper clipping on the subject

It is not unwise then to say
that the air is hung close with diamonds
that we breathe diamond
our lungs hoarding, exchanging
our blood sowing them rich and thick
along every course it takes
Does this explain
why some of us are so hard
why some of us shine
why we are all precious

that we are awash in creation
spumed with diamonds
shot through with beauty
that survived the deaths of stars

Salvation

George Ella Lyon

"What does the Lord want with Virgil's heart?
And what is Virgil going to do without one?"

O Lord, spare him the Call.
You're looking for bass
in a pond stocked with catfish.
Pass him by.
You got our best.
You took Mammy and the truck and the second hay.
What do You want with Virgil's heart?

Virgil, he comes in of a night
so wore out he can hardly chew
blacked with dust that don't come off at the bathhouse.
He washes again
eats onions and beans with the rest of us
then gives the least one a shoulder ride to bed
slow and singing
    Down in some lone valley
    in some lonesome place
    where the wild birds do whistle . . .

After that, he sags like a full feed sack
on a couch alongside the TV
and watches whatever news Your waves are giving.
His soul sifts out
like feed from a slit in that sack
and he's gone
wore out and give out and plumb used up Lord.
What do You want with his heart?

The Foot-Washing
George Ella Lyon

"I wouldn't take the bread and wine if I didn't wash feet."
Old Regular Baptist

They kneel on the slanting floor
before feet white as roots.
humble as tree stumps.
Men before men
women before women
to soothe the sourness
bound in each other's journeys.
Corns, calluses, bone knobs
all received and rinsed
given back clean
to Sunday shoes and hightops.

This is how they prepare
for the Lord's Supper,
singing and carrying a towel
and a basin of water,
praying while kids put soot
in their socks—almost as good
as nailing someone in the outhouse.

Jesus started it: He washed feet
after Magdalen dried His ankles
with her hair. "If I wash thee not,
thou hast no part with me."

All servants, they bathe
flesh warped to its balance.
God of the rootwad,
Lord of the bucket in the well.

Nightingales in America
Jane Flanders

The older women were Sunbeams and I guess we
were Cherubs or Lambs but our mothers were Nightingales.
Sunday mornings they prayed and sang in a niche
of the Methodist Church. They studied the sorrows of Jesus
and all who suffered in places like Abyssinia,
where there was still so much to be done.
There was much to be done everywhere, of course—
bake sales, suppers, altars, the homely chores
women were made for. Once a year, however,
they paused in their good works and took us all
to Cold Spring Park. After we skidded around
the roller rink maybe a million times,
seesawed, swang, got skinned and bitten, skittered
through poison ivy, fell in the creek, rode
the little train and ate our fill we lay back
blissfully in the grass and watched our blessed
mothers, their wings suddenly tinged with gold,
wheel overhead in the shape of a cross, singing
a wistful hymn we never could remember.

The Pedestrian Woman
Robin Morgan

She stands at the intersection, waiting
to stride across in that inimitable way of hers,
shoulderbag banging against one hip, head high,
her hair promiscuous to the wind.

Or sits at the typewriter, inconspicuous
as any other woman,
writing messages to the universe
which will get her in trouble with the boss.

No past, no future, flickers like a clue
in all those chance encounters
that accumulate a life.

See her ride the subway. See her
warm the leftovers for her supper.
See her feed her dog.
And can you see what vision
fires its shape in her sleep's kiln,
what passion, irony, and wit,
what love, what courage
are disguised
in all her daily movements?

Ordinary is a word that has no meaning.

Her life is a fine piece of Japanese pottery
in the Shibui style,
so crafted that to see the cup's exterior
is to be privy only to its dull sienna clay
and to the flavored warmth with which you choose to fill it.

But drained of all your preconceptions
you may discover the bowl inside—
a high-glazed hyacinth blue
that rushes to your heart
and there remains, like an indelible message
you remember from a fortune told in tea leaves once,
like a wet jasmine flower
that you can never rinse away.

Love Should Grow Up Like a Wild Iris in the Fields

Susan Griffin

Love should grow up like a wild iris in the fields,
unexpected, after a terrible storm, opening a purple
mouth to the rain, with not a thought to the future,
ignorant of the grass and the graveyard of leaves
around, forgetting its own beginning. Love should
grow like a wild iris
but does not.
Love more often is to be found in kitchens at the dinner
    hour,
tired out and hungry, lingers over tables in houses where
the walls record movements; while the cook is probably
    angry,
and the ingredients of the meal are budgeted, while
a child cries feed me now and her mother not quite
hysterical says over and over, wait just a bit, just a bit,
love should grow up in the fields like a wild iris
but never does
really startle anyone, was to be expected, was to be
predicted, is almost absurd, goes on from day to day, not
    quite
blindly, gets taken to the cleaners every fall, sings old
songs over and over, and falls on the same piece of rug
    that
never gets tacked down, gives up, wants to hide, is not
brave, knows too much, is not like an
iris growing wild but more like
staring into space
in the street
not quite sure
which door it was, annoyed about the sidewalk being
slippery, trying all the doors, thinking
if love wished the world to be well, it would be well.
Love should
grow up like a wild iris, but doesn't, it comes from
the midst of everything else, sees like the iris
of an eye, when the light is right,
feels in blindness and when there is nothing else is
tender, blinks, and opens
face up to the skies.

Miracle

Susan Griffin

It all happened on the water
Jesus' walking
the fishermen watching
from their boats.
When they picked up their nets
they half expected
a miraculous catch
but it was as ordinary
as the rest of the day.
Only some of them understood.
This is how it always is
with a vision.
Jesus walked on the water
only once.
This wasn't science.
What was it the fishermen were
supposed to see.
A man moving over the surface
of the sea as if it were
some other substance like ground.
Was this all there was?
Picture yourself
you are out there on the water
you look at the horizon.
You are so used to seeing that part
of the sky it's become
part of your eyes.
Then you blink, staring
you turn to shake your companion.
This was not what you expected to see.
Not even what you wished for.
What difference does it make
a man walking on the water?
But even so the day
going on as it usually does
is cut with a certain clarity
and you, you feel an inexplicable
happiness, the water
beneath you, the
bright air above.

The Woman's Bible (excerpt)
Elizabeth Cady Stanton

I think that the doctrine of the Virgin birth as something higher, sweeter, nobler than ordinary motherhood, is a slur on all the natural motherhood of the world. I believe that millions of children have been as immaculately conceived, as purely born, as was the Nazarene. Why not? Out of this doctrine, and that which is akin to it, have sprung all the monasteries and the nunneries of the world, which have disgraced and distorted and demoralized manhood and womanhood for a thousand years. I place beside the false, monkish, unnatural claim of the Immaculate Conception my mother, who was as holy in her motherhood as was Mary herself.

how he is coming then
Lucille Clifton

like a pot turned on the straw
nuzzled by cows and an old man
dressed like a father. like a loaf
a poor baker sets in the haystack to cool.
like a shepherd who hears in his herding
his mother whisper   my son   my son.

Revolutionary Patience (excerpt)
Dorothee Sölle

He gave answers to questions they didn't ask
sometimes they didn't dare
open their mouths anymore
not because they hadn't understood
he was taking from them
everything sacred and safe
he offered no guarantees

Fire was not sacred to him or neon
not singing or silence
not fornication or chastity
in his speech foxes breaddough
and much mended nets became sacred
the down and out were his proof
and actually he had as much assurance
of victory as we in these parts do

None

Holy the Firm (excerpt)
Annie Dillard

There is one church here, so I go to it. On Sunday mornings I quit the house and wander down the hill to the white frame church in the firs. On a big Sunday there might be twenty of us there; often I am the only person under sixty, and feel as though I'm on an archaeological tour of Soviet Russia. The members are of mixed denominations; the minister is a Congregationalist, and wears a white shirt. The man knows God. Once, in the middle of the long pastoral prayer of intercession for the whole world—for the gift of wisdom to its leaders, for hope and mercy to the grieving and pained, succor to the op-pressed, and God's grace to all—in the middle of this he stopped, and burst out, "Lord, we bring you these same petitions every week." After a shocked pause, he continued reading the prayer. Because of this, I like him very much. "Good morning!" he says after the first hymn and invocation, startling me witless every time, and we all shout back, "Good morning!"

The churchwomen all bring flowers for the altar; they haul in arrange-ments as big as hedges, of wayside herbs in season, and flowers from their gardens, huge bunches of foliage and blossoms as tall as I am, in vases the size of tubs, and the altar still looks empty, irredeemably linoleum, and beige. We had a wretched singer once, a guest from a Canadian congregation, a hulking blond girl with chopped hair and big shoulders, who wore tinted spectacles and a long lacy dress, and sang, grinning, to faltering accompaniment, an entirely secular song about mountains. Nothing could have been more appar-ent than that God loved this girl; nothing could more surely convince me of God's unending mercy than the continued existence on earth of the church.

Garlic
Jeanne Foster

The way in is only hinted at,
a crevice between cloves,
a darkness, revealed
by the ripping away of the papery
layers of husk, flipped up
like a girl's hair.
In there, it could be thighs,
lying in the clean curves
of Arctic banks; it could be
a sepia enlargement of a familiar
but unidentifiable detail
of the human form; it
could be one of Georgia O'Keefe's
desert bones or the very insides
of a calla lily or the ivory
shadow within an intricate Chinese
carving. It could be the tooth
of the tooth fairy. It could be the night
that lies between two words.

Welcome Morning
Anne Sexton

There is joy
in all:
in the hair I brush each morning,
in the Cannon towel, newly washed,
that I rub my body with each morning,
in the chapel of eggs I cook
each morning,
in the outcry from the kettle
that heats my coffee
each morning,
in the spoon and the chair
that cry "hello there, Anne"

each morning,
in the godhead of the table
that I set my silver, plate, cup upon
each morning.

All this is God,
right here in my pea-green house
each morning
and I mean,
though often forget,
to give thanks,
to faint down by the kitchen table
in a prayer of rejoicing
as the holy birds at the kitchen window
peck into their marriage of seeds.

So while I think of it,
let me paint a thank-you on my palm
for this God, this laughter of the morning,
lest it go unspoken.

The Joy that isn't shared, I've heard,
dies young.

domestic poem
Eileen Moeller

nightfall I sink
into dishwash meditation
steaming china prayer wheels
crystalline bells of the lost horizon
crockery mandalas
chanting din and lull of running water
breathing slows
moist heat muscles soften
zen poems drip from silverware
my air humming out
in a cleansing melody
washing the frantic stew of a whole day
down the drain

along with the suds
those transient rainbow things
with the thin skin of
a passing instant.

Beatitude
Claire Bateman

Blessed are the flabby people at Walgreen's
buying Trojan transparent ribbed golden condoms.

Unlike the couple on the package,
they have never had
a beach encounter at sunset.

They are landlocked.
They have shoveled their weight in worries
and are well acquainted with mulch.

They have problems with flatulence
because they fry with lard.

Yet darkness
rocks their unfashionable limbs
into phosphorescence.

In that tide they overcome gravity.
Holy, they vocalize with the whales.

How to Stuff a Pepper
Nancy Willard

Now, said the cook, I will teach you
how to stuff a pepper with rice.

Take your pepper green, and gently,
for peppers are shy. No matter which side

you approach, it's always the backside.
Perched on green buttocks, the pepper sleeps.
In its silk tights, it dreams
of somersaults and parsley,
of the days when the sexes were one.

Slash open the sleeve
as if you were cutting a paper lantern,
and enter a moon, spilled like a melon,
a fever of pearls,
a conversation of glaciers.
It is a temple built to the worship
of morning light.

I have sat under the great globe
of seeds on the roof of that chamber,
too dazzled to gather the taste I came for.
I have taken the pepper in hand,
smooth and blind, a runt in the rich
evolution of roses and ferns.
You say I have not yet taught you

to stuff a pepper?
Cooking takes time.

Next time we'll consider the rice.

The Spirit and the Flesh Are One

The cultural resistance to embracing the sensual and the erotic as part of our spiritual nature is exceedingly strong. We in this country spend an inordinate amount of time attempting to control our bodies. Objectified, surveyed, judged, our flesh is seen as an instrument, a means to various and sundry ends. The hair shirts of yore have become the exercise bikes of today. In the following selections, that traditional Western division of spirit and flesh breaks down. The flesh is not just a conduit for the holy: the flesh is holy. We can rejoice in it.

Julian of Norwich

I understood that
our sensuality is grounded
in Nature, in Compassion
and in Grace.
This enables us to receive
gifts that lead to
everlasting life.
For I saw that in our sensuality
God is.
For God is never out of
the soul.

To praise
Ellen Bass

I want to praise bodies
nerves and synapses
the impulse that travels the spine
    like fish darting

I want to praise the mouth
that warm wet lair where the tongue reclines
and the tongue, roused
    slithering a cool path

I want to praise hands
those architects that create us anew
fingers, cartographers, revealing
    who we can become
and palms, cupped priestesses
    worshipping the long slow curve

I want to praise muscle
and the heart, that flamboyant champion
    with its insistent pelting like
    tropical rain

Hair, the sweep of it
   a breeze

and feet, arch taut
   stretching like cats

I want to praise the face, engraved
like a river bed; it breaks like morning
   like a piñata, festival of hope

Breasts, cornucopia
nipples that jump up, gleeful
   like a child greeting the day

and clitoris, shimmering
a huge tender pearl
   in that succulent oyster

I want to praise the love cries
sharp, brilliant as ice
and the roar that swells in the lungs
   like an avalanche

I want to praise the gush, the hot
spring thaw of it, the rivers
   wild with it

Bodies, our extravagant bodies

And I want to praise you, how you have
lavished yours
upon mine
   until I want to praise

In Celebration of My Uterus
Anne Sexton

Everyone in me is a bird.
I am beating all my wings.
They wanted to cut you out
but they will not.

They said you were immeasurably empty
but you are not.
They said you were sick unto dying
but they were wrong.
You are singing like a school girl.
You are not torn.

Sweet weight,
in celebration of the woman I am
and of the soul of the woman I am
and of the central creature and its delight
I sing for you. I dare to live.
Hello, spirit. Hello, cup.
Fasten, cover. Cover that does contain.
Hello to the soil of the fields.
Welcome, roots.

Each cell has a life.
There is enough here to please a nation.
It is enough that the populace own these goods.
Any person, any commonwealth would say of it,
"It is good this year that we may plant again
and think forward to a harvest.
A blight had been forecast and has been cast out."
Many women are singing together of this:
one is in a shoe factory cursing the machine,
one is at the aquarium tending a seal,
one is dull at the wheel of her Ford,
one is at the toll gate collecting,
one is tying the cord of a calf in Arizona,
one is straddling a cello in Russia,
one is shifting pots on the stove in Egypt,
one is painting her bedroom walls moon color,
one is dying but remembering a breakfast,
one is stretching on her mat in Thailand,
one is wiping the ass of her child,
one is staring out the window of a train
in the middle of Wyoming and one is
anywhere and some are everywhere and all
seem to be singing, although some can not
sing a note.

Sweet weight,
in celebration of the woman I am
let me carry a ten-foot scarf,

let me drum for the nineteen-year-olds,
let me carry bowls for the offering
(if that is my part).
Let me study the cardiovascular tissue,
let me examine the angular distance of meteors,
let me suck on the stems of flowers
(if that is my part).
Let me make certain tribal figures
(if that is my part).
For this thing the body needs
let me sing
for the supper,
for the kissing,
for the correct
yes.

Use of the Erotic: The Erotic as Power (excerpt)
Audre Lorde

The erotic functions for me in several ways, and the first is in the power which comes from sharing deeply any pursuit with another person. The sharing of joy, whether physical, emotional, psychic or intellectual, forms a bridge between the sharers which can be the basis for understanding much of what is not shared between them, and lessens the threat of their difference.

Another important way in which the erotic connection functions is the open and fearless underlining of my capacity for joy. In the way my body stretches to music and opens into response, hearkening to its deepest rhythms, so every level upon which I sense also opens to the erotically satisfying experience, whether it is dancing, building a bookcase, writing a poem, examining an idea.

That self-connection shared is a measure of the joy which I know myself to be capable of feeling, a reminder of my capacity for feeling. And that deep and irreplaceable knowledge of my capacity for joy comes to demand from all of my life that it be lived within the knowledge that such satisfaction is possible, and does not have to be called marriage, nor god, nor an afterlife.

This is one reason why the erotic is so feared, and so often relegated to the bedroom alone, when it is recognized at all. For once we begin to feel deeply all the aspects of our lives, we begin to demand from ourselves and from our lives pursuits that they feel in accordance with that joy which we know ourselves to be capable of. Our erotic knowledge empowers us, becomes a lens through which we scrutinize all aspects of our existence, forcing

ourselves to evaluate those aspects honestly in terms of their relative meaning
within our lives. And this is a grave responsibility, projected from within each
of us, not to settle for the convenient, the shoddy, the conventionally expected, nor the merely safe.

Revolutionary Patience (excerpt)
Dorothee Sölle

I don't as they put it believe in god
but to him I cannot say no hard as I try
take a look at him in the garden
when his friends ran out on him
his face wet with fear
and with the spit of his enemies
him I have to believe

Him I can't bear to abandon
to the great disregard for life
to the monotonous passing of millions of years
to the moronic rhythm of work leisure and work
to the boredom we fail to dispel
in cars in beds in stores

That's how it is they say what do you want
uncertain and not uncritically
I subscribe to the other hypothesis
which is his story
that's not how it is he said for god is
and he staked his life on this claim

Thinking about it I find
one can't let him pay alone
for his hypothesis
so I believe him about
god

The way one believes another's laughter
his tears
or marriage or no for an answer
that's how you'll learn
to believe him about life
promised to all

God send easter
Lucille Clifton

and we will lace the
jungle on
and step out
brilliant as birds
against the concrete country
feathers waving as we
dance toward jesus
sun reflecting mango
and apple as we
glory in our skin

spring song
Lucille Clifton

the green of Jesus
is breaking the ground
and the sweet
smell of delicious Jesus
is opening the house and
the dance of Jesus music
has hold of the air and
the world is turning
in the body of Jesus and
the future is possible

The Network of the Imaginary Mother (excerpt)
Robin Morgan

As it was in the beginning,
   I say:
   Here is your sacrament—

      Take. Eat. This is my body,
      this real milk, thin, sweet, bluish,

which I give for the life of the world.
Like sap to spring it rises
even before the first faint cry is heard,
an honest nourishment
alone able to sustain you.

I say:
Here is your eternal testament—

This cup, this chalice, this primordial cauldron
of real menstrual blood
the color of clay warm with promise,
rhythmic, cyclical, fit for lining the uterus
and shed for many,
for the remission of living.

Here is your bread of life.
Here is the blood by which you live in me.

Meditations with Hildegard of Bingen (excerpt)
Hildegard of Bingen

The soul is kissed by God
in its innermost regions.

With interior yearning,
grace and blessing
are bestowed.

It is a yearning to take on God's
    gentle yoke,
it is a yearning to give one's self
    to God's way.

Saturday Night Worship
Ann Carhart

We talk about God
by the bed.
I light candles
for our sacramental rites.
We love
and remember those women
no church would commemorate.
Sheets we warm again
cool slowly.
Night hangs around for a long time.
God yawns
and the dawn comes
reluctantly
while I want
to gather up
our night music
like an armful of flowers and
toss one note at a time
through the skylight
to mingle
with the ringing Sunday bells.

White Petticoats
Chana Bloch

for Ariel

If the egg had one spot of blood on it
the rabbis said, Throw it away!
As if they could legislate

perfection.
Dress the bride in white
petticoats! Let there be

no stain
on your ceremony! As if
we could keep our lives

from spilling
on our new clothes. That night
we came home

strangers, too tired
for words,
fog in the high trees

and a trunk full of shiny boxes
we didn't unwrap.
There's a bravery

in being naked.
We left our clothes
on the doorknob, the floor, the bed,

and a live moon
opened its arms around
the speckled dark.

O Taste and See

Denise Levertov

The world is
not with us enough.
O taste and see

the subway Bible poster said,
meaning **The Lord**, meaning
if anything all that lives
to the imagination's tongue,

grief, mercy, language,
tangerine, weather, to
breathe them, bite,
savor, chew, swallow, transform

into our flesh our
deaths, crossing the street, plum, quince,
living in the orchard and being

hungry, and plucking
the fruit.

Common Prayer
Lynn Ungar

Sunday morning at the marina
Barely enough wind to keep the kites aloft
and so we drifted to the ground
to nibble bagels, chocolate,
giant loose-skinned oranges,
random poetry, blades of grass
Sacraments and indulgences
for the first of Spring

And in the moment before sleep
my breast against your arm
sang *Gloria*
and the soles of my feet
cried *Sanctus* to the sun
Placing the last chocolate
in your mouth I whispered
"This is my body, take and eat"
and we melted   very slowly
on the earth's tongue

Catechism

Betsy Sholl

I begin as tradition advises
with a question for the rabbi.
How can the soul be free of its body?

But God knows they haven't ordained women long.
Her eyes are still bright. She leans forward,
peers into mine. Why would you want to?

Because it's there to be climbed.
Because I'm nearly forty and it's getting harder
to stay thin, wake rested, not weep in the afternoon.
It says *shame*, and *eat*. It's an imbecile
rocking itself at 5 in the morning
as if wind had no sway, trees turning above us
in March air so wild you know the invisible exists.

She leans back. I can't tell if she smiles
or frowns. What makes you want to see the invisible?
How would you know wind without flesh, hair?

I would be wind, I say.
But now this rabbi in woman form looks hard at me:
Then wind would change into fire.
You torture yourself.

But the body slumps and whines.
It's a dog, I say.

Her ears prick up. I know what she's thinking.
So feed it, she smiles. Let it keep you warm.
At night when its legs twitch, when a sound
breaks from its throat and wakes you,
listen.

Sunrise
Mary Oliver

You can
die for it—
an idea,
or the world. People

have done so,
brilliantly,
letting
their small bodies be bound

to the stake,
creating
an unforgettable
fury of light. But

this morning,
climbing the familiar hills
in the familiar
fabric of dawn, I thought

of China,
and India
and Europe, and I thought
how the sun

blazes
for everyone just
so joyfully
as it rises

under the lashes
of my own eyes, and I thought
I am so many!
What is my name?

What is the name
of the deep breath I would take
over and over
for all of us? Call it

whatever you want, it is
happiness, it is another one
of the ways to enter
fire.

Adam Says See (excerpt)
Julia Randall

How shall we walk naked when
all our dress and all our skin
name us thick or thin?
How shall I my brother tell
underneath his coat of mail,
or my sister in her furs?
How shall I forget my eyes?

One way, two ways:
sing the dark its name,
or walk about the street of day
teaching every passerby
Adam's genealogy.

The Unity of All That Is

Mystics from various religious traditions have in common the experience of feeling themselves one with all else that exists. That spirit prevails in the following selections. The writers acknowledge the oneness, the ultimate lack of separation, of the mystic tradition. They suggest that the creation of "the other" is a false dichotomy that will in fact keep us from love and compassion for others and from the deepest understanding of self.

Our Houses

Linda Hogan

When we enter the unknown
of our houses,
go inside the given up dark
and sheltering walls alone
and turn out the lamps
we fall bone to bone in bed.

Neighbors, the old woman who knows you
turns over in me
and I wake up
another country. There's no more
north and south.
Asleep, we pass through one another
like blowing snow,
all of us,
all.

Subway

Susan Fawcett

We speed through tunnels under the frozen ground
rocking side to side in rows.
Wheels rumble and crash, smoke drifts over us
and someone's odor like terrible cheese.
Our faces lift as if transcending—
the shabby man whose eyes roll upward
reading advertisements against his will,
the young Hispanic mother, tranced,
patting her parcel of pink blankets.
Perhaps she is in Santo Domingo,
a small yard she knew as a girl,
tinsel decorations blowing in the sun.

Here, angry signatures of children
throb in their haloes of spray paint,
red and black, big as false gods.
We stare as hewn stone walls flash past

and vaulted arches stained with water
like lost temples half-perceived,
not understood, blurred rows of columns
holding only the load of the city.
Now we are down to the level of grief,
swaying together, sleeve to sleeve,
carried fast, packed tight
as shoots in a flat. This is as close
as we come to bedrock, soil. In each of us
a dark node opens like hunger.

Mrs. Schneider in Church
Kathleen Norris

"The Christian religion is a singing faith."
—Presbyterian hymnal

It's the willingness to sing
that surprises me:
out of tune,
we drag the organist along
and sing, knowing we can't,
and our quite ordinary voices
carry us over.

I get caught up
in the parts:
the tenor to my left,
still clear and high,
proving that voice
is no clue to character.
I see him not in that brown suit
but in shirtsleeves
in the back room
of his farm-parts store,
cheating at cards,
his wife up front, ragged with work.

That complaining soprano
above the rest
is the grocer's widow.
She never stopped screaming at him,
and hates him now
for dying.

Every week
the young wives lead us,
tilting forward in improbable shoes:
they're firmly anchored
by the wobbly bass
behind me.
When I was such a one,
still slender and moist-looking,
he attacked me in the coal cellar
and I fought him off
with a shovel.

Now we are changed,
making a noise
greater than ourselves,
to be worthy of the lesson:
all duly noted,
all forgiven.

Mass for the Day of St. Thomas Didymus (excerpt)
Denise Levertov

Powers and principalities—all the gods,
angels and demigods, eloquent animals, oracles,
storms of blessing and wrath—

> all that Imagination
> has wrought, has rendered,
> striving, in throes of epiphany—

> naming, forming—to give
> to the Vast Loneliness
> a hearth, a locus—

send forth their song towards
the harboring silence, uttering
the ecstasy of their names, the multiform
name of the Other, the known
Unknown, unknowable:

sanctus, hosanna, sanctus.

29.

Alta

the man standing next to molten steel.
boy, i wouldnt do that.
the woman raising seven children.
there are many kinds of courage & i
dont have them all.
we're all in this together.

there's an earwig under the spoon.
not only am i going to let it live,
i'm not even going to put it "outside".
"let it live". i actually said that.
shake hands with god.

The Way of All Ideology (excerpt)
Susan Griffin

I have encountered the idea of a denied self before. Writing of racism in the 1960s, James Baldwin spoke in *The Fire Next Time* of the creation of the "nigger" in the white mind. The idea of the nigger, he observed, said nothing about black character and everything about white racist character. The nigger is the denied part of the white idea of self, a fantasy of another's being created out of a purposeful ignorance of the self. And I discovered the same delusion, the same denied self, in the pornographer's idea of a woman.

Moreover, as I wrote about the pornographer's mind I discovered that pornography itself was not so much an art form as it was an ideology and an

ideology which, like the ideology of racism, *requires* the creation of another, a
not-I, an enemy. This is a world view in which the self is irrevocably split so
that it does not recognize its other half, and in which all phenomena, experience, and human qualities are also split into the superior and the inferior, the
righteous and the evil, the above and the below. What is superior, according
to this ideology, is by rights above all that is inferior. For the righteous must
have authority over and control of the evil.

And the other, the not-I, bears all those qualities which are lesser and
bad; thus the other is the enemy who must be controlled or annihilated.

*

I can be angry. I can hate. I can rage. But the moment I have defined
another being as my enemy, I lose part of myself, the complexity and subtlety
of my vision. I begin to exist in a closed system. When anything goes wrong,
I blame my enemy. If I wake troubled, my enemy had led me to this feeling. If
I cannot sleep, it is because of my enemy. Slowly all the power in my life
begins to be located outside, and my whole being is defined in relation to this
outside force, which becomes daily more monstrous, more evil, more laden
with all the qualities in myself I no longer wish to own. The quality of my
thought then is diminished. My imagination grows small. My self seems mea-
gre. For my enemy has stolen all these.

The Sabbath of Mutual Respect
Marge Piercy

In the natural year come two thanksgivings,
the harvest of summer and the harvest of fall,
two times when we eat and drink and remember our dead
under the golden basin of the moon of plenty.

Abundance, Habondia, food for the winter,
too much now and survival later. After
the plant bears, it dies into seed.
The blowing grasses nourish us, wheat
and corn and rye, millet and rice, oat
and barley and buckwheat, all the serviceable
grasses of the pasture that the cow grazes,
the lamb, the horse, the goat; the grasses
that quicken into meat and cheese and milk,
the humble necessary mute vegetable bees,

the armies of the grasses waving their
golden banners of ripe seed.
                    The sensual
round fruit that gleams with the sun
stored in its sweetness.
                    The succulent
ephemera of the summer garden, bloodwarm
tomatoes, tender small squash, crisp
beans, the milky corn, the red peppers
exploding like cherry bombs in the mouth.

We praise abundance by eating of it,
reveling in choice on a table set with roses
and lilies and phlox, zucchini and lettuce
and eggplant before the long winter
of root crops.
                    Fertility and choice:
every row dug in spring means weeks
of labor. Plant too much and the seedlings
choke in weeds as the warm rain soaks them.
The goddess of abundance Habondia is also
the spirit of labor and choice.
                    In another
life, dear sister, I too would bear six fat
children. In another life, my sister, I too
would love another woman and raise one child
together as if that pushed from both our wombs.
In another life, sister, I too would dwell
solitary and splendid as a lighthouse on the rocks
or be born to mate for life like the faithful goose.
Praise all our choices. Praise any woman
who chooses, and make safe her choice.

Habondia, Artemis, Cybele, Demeter, Ishtar,
Aphrodite, Au Set, Hecate, Themis, Lilith,
Thea, Gaia, Bridgit, The Great Grandmother of Us
All, Yemanja, Cerridwen, Freya, Corn Maiden,
Mawu, Amaterasu, Maires, Nut, Spider-Woman,
Neith, Au Zit, Hathor, Inanna, Shin Moo,
Diti, Arinna, Anath, Tiamat, Astoreth:
the names flesh out our histories, our choices,
our passions and what we will never embody
but pass by with respect. When I consecrate
my body in the temple of our history,

when I pledge myself to remain empty
and clear for the voices coming through
I do not choose for you or lessen your choice.

Habondia, the real abundance, is the power
to say yes and to say no, to open
and to close, to take or to leave
and not to be taken by force or law
or fear or poverty or hunger.
To bear children or not to bear by choice
is holy. To bear children unwanted
is to be used like a public sewer.
To be sterilized unchosen is to have
your heart cut out. To love women
is holy and holy is the free love of men
and precious to live taking whichever comes
and precious to live unmated as a peachtree.

Praise the lives you did not choose.
They will heal you, tell your story, fight
for you. You eat the bread of their labor.
You drink the wine of their joy. I tell you
after I went under the surgeon's knife
for the laparoscopy I felt like a trumpet
an Amazon was blowing sonorous charges on.
Then my womb learned to open on the full
moon without pain and my pleasure deepened
till my body shuddered like troubled water.
When my friend gave birth I held her in joy
as the child's head thrust from her vagina
like the sun rising at dawn wet and red.

Praise our choices, sisters, for each doorway
open to us was taken by squads of fighting
women who paid years of trouble and struggle,
who paid their wombs, their sleep, their lives
that we might walk through these gates upright.
Doorways are sacred to women for we
are the doorways of life and we must choose
what comes in and what goes out. Freedom
is our real abundance.

Chains of Fire (excerpt)
Elsa Gidlow

I know myself linked by chains of fires
To every woman who has kept a hearth.
In the resinous smoke
I smell hut, castle, cave,
Mansion and hovel,
See in the shifting flame my mother
And grandmothers out over the world.

Dream 2: Brian the Still-Hunter
Margaret Atwood

The man I saw in the forest
used to come to our house
every morning, never said anything;
I learned from the neighbours later
he once tried to cut his throat.

I found him at the end of the path
sitting on a fallen tree
cleaning his gun.

There was no wind;
around us the leaves rustled.

He said to me:
I kill because I have to

but every time I aim, I feel
my skin grow fur
my head heavy with antlers
and during the stretched instant
the bullet glides on its thread of speed
my soul runs innocent as hooves.

Is God just to his creatures?

I die more often than many.

He looked up and I saw
the white scar made by the hunting knife
around his neck.

When I woke
I remembered: he has been gone
twenty years and not heard from.

cutting greens
Lucille Clifton

curling them around
i hold their bodies in obscene embrace
thinking of everything but kinship.
collards and kale
strain against each strange other
away from my kissmaking hand and
the iron bedpot.
the pot is black,
the cutting board is black,
my hand,
and just for a minute
the greens roll black under the knife,
and the kitchen twists dark on its spine
and i taste in my natural appetite
the bond of live things everywhere.

The House That Fear Built: Warsaw, 1943
Jane Flanders

*"The purpose of poetry is to remind us how difficult it is to remain just
one person, for our house is open, there are no keys in the doors."*
—Czeslaw Milosz

I am the boy with his hands raised over his head
in Warsaw.

I am the soldier whose rifle is trained
on the boy with his hands raised over his head
in Warsaw.

I am the woman with lowered gaze
who fears the soldier whose rifle is trained
on the boy with his hands raised over his head
in Warsaw.

I am the man in the overcoat
who loves the woman with lowered gaze
who fears the soldier whose rifle is trained
on the boy with his hands raised over his head
in Warsaw.

I am the stranger who photographs
the man in the overcoat
who loves the woman with lowered gaze
who fears the soldier whose rifle is trained
on the boy with his hands raised over his head
in Warsaw.

The crowd, of which I am each part, moves on
beneath my window, for I am the crone too
who shakes her sheets
over every street in the world
muttering
What's this? What's this?

A Ceremony (excerpt)
Robin Morgan

We will grow old, and older.
One of us will die, and then the other.
The earth itself will be impaled
on sunspokes. It doesn't matter.
We have been imprinted on the protons
of energy herself,

and so stand in another atmosphere,
where an undiscovered star we will never live to see
casts shadows on a grove of succulents we cannot yet imagine.
There our interchangeable features still vibrate and blur,
each smile half of one circle,

each utterance spiraling like light
upward in shudders along the spine
as if the moon and you and I were slivers
of one mirror, gazing on herself at last.

Childhood of a Stranger
Claire Bateman

You too once were carried in your sleep—
you to someone a warm weight of breath and cloth,
wisps of sleep like slow steam off your seamless face,
day distilling into dreams in a skull yet soft.
Now we are encrusted with barbed years,
flinty, adamanatine, ready to repel
all assaults against our independence.
But for that hint of honey, trace of down,
that secret nerve that never has grown numb,
there is a debt between us even now
that our autonomy cannot remove:
a bent toward something more than tolerance,
older than kindness, oddly akin to love.

Dancing with Poets
Ellen Bryant Voigt

"The accident" is what he calls the time
he threw himself from a window four floors up,
breaking his back and both ankles, so that walking
became the direst labor for this man
who takes my hand, invites me to the empty strip of floor
that fronts the instruments, a length of polished wood
the shape of a grave. *Unsuited for this world*—
his body bears the marks of it, his hand
is tense with effort and with shame, and I shy away
from any audience, but I love to dance, and soon
we find a way to move, drifting apart as each

effects a different ripple across the floor,
a plaid and a stripe to match the solid navy of the band.
And suddenly the band is getting better, so pleased
to have this pair of dancers, since we make evident
the music in the noise—and the dull pulse
leaps with unexpected riffs and turns, we can hear
how good the keyboard really is, the bright cresting
of another major key as others join us: a strict
block of a man, a formidable cliff of mind, dancing
as if melted, as if unhinged; his partner a gift of brave
elegance to those who watch her dance; and at her elbow,
Berryman back from the bridge, and Frost, relieved
of grievances, Dickinson waltzing there with lavish Keats,
who coughs into a borrowed handkerchief—all the poets of exile
and despair, unfit for this life, all those who cannot speak
but only sing, all those who cannot walk
who strut and spin until the waiting citizens at the bar,
aloof, judgmental, begin to sway or drum their straws
or hum, leave their seats to crowd the narrow floor
and now we are one body, sweating and foolish,
one body with its clear pathetic grace, not
lifted out of grief but dancing it, transforming
for one night this local bar, before we're turned back out
to our separate selves, to the dangerous streets and houses,
to the overwhelming drone of the living world.

Remember

Joy Harjo

Remember the sky that you were born under,
know each of the star's stories.
Remember the moon, know who she is. I met her
in a bar once in Iowa City.
Remember the sun's birth at dawn, that is the
strongest point of time. Remember sundown
and the giving away to night.
Remember your birth, how your mother struggled
to give you form and breath. You are evidence of
her life, and her mother's, and hers.
Remember your father. He is your life, also.
Remember the earth whose skin you are:

red earth, black earth, yellow earth, white earth
brown earth, we are earth.
Remember the plants, trees, animal life who all have their
tribes, their families, their histories, too. Talk to them,
listen to them. They are alive poems.
Remember the wind. Remember her voice. She knows the
origin of this universe. I heard her singing Kiowa war
dance songs at the corner of Fourth and Central once.
Remember that you are all people and that all people
are you.
Remember that you are this universe and that this
universe is you.
Remember that all is in motion, is growing, is you.
Remember that language comes from this.
Remember the dance that language is, that life is.
Remember.

Untitled poem from "The Dinner Party"
Judy Chicago

And then all that has divided us will merge
And then compassion will be wedded to power
And then softness will come to a world that is harsh
        and unkind
And then both men and women will be gentle
And then both women and men will be strong
And then no person will be subject to another's will
And then all will be rich and free and varied
And then the greed of some will give way to the needs
        of many
And then all will share equally in the Earth's
        abundance
And then all will care for the sick and the weak
        and the old
And then all will nourish the young
And then all will cherish life's creatures
And then all will live in harmony with each other
        and the Earth
And then everywhere will be called Eden once again

Images of the Divine

God is a spirit, a mystery beyond human understanding, and therefore we can only approach that mystery through metaphor. Our metaphors come, of course, from human and cultural understandings of the good, the loving, the just. The problem is that in the formulation of the religious metaphors we live by, women's experience has once again been largely discounted: God has been king, prince, lord, father, conqueror, judge. In the selections that follow, the image of God is evoked in surprising and rewarding forms: a mother cat, a blossom pressed in a book, a gardener, a veiled woman, a new-born lamb. Such images allow a divinity of softness and vulnerability, of tenderness and nurturance. We are led to less fear and to more comfort and hope than traditional images alone have provided.

Briefly It Enters, and Briefly Speaks

Jane Kenyon

I am the blossom pressed in a book
and found again after 200 years . . .

I am the maker, the lover, and the keeper . . .

When the young girl who starves
sits down to a table
she will sit beside me . . .

I am food on the prisoner's plate . . .

I am water rushing to the wellhead,
filling the pitcher until it spills . . .

I am the patient gardener
of the dry and weedy garden . . .

I am the stone step,
the latch, and the working hinge . . .

I am the heart contracted by joy . . .
the longest hair, white
before the rest . . .

I am the basket of fruit
presented to the widow . . .

I am the musk rose opening
unattended, the fern on the boggy summit . . .

I am the one whose love
overcomes you, already with you
when you think to call my name. . . .

The Bat
Jane Kenyon

I was reading about rationalism,
the kind of thing we do up north
in early winter, where the sun
leaves work for the day at 4:15.

Maybe the world *is* intelligible
to the rational mind:
and maybe we light the lamps at dusk
for nothing. . . .

Then I heard wings overhead.

The cats and I chased the bat
in circles—living room, kitchen,
pantry, kitchen, living room. . . .
At every turn it evaded us

like the identity of the third person
in the Trinity: the one
who spoke through the prophets,
the one who astounded Mary
by suddenly coming near.

Beyond God the Father (excerpt)
Mary Daly

Why indeed must "God" be a noun? Why not a verb—the most active and dynamic of all? Hasn't the naming of "God" as a noun been an act of murdering that dynamic Verb? And isn't the Verb infinitely more personal than a mere static noun? The anthropomorphic symbols for God may be intended to convey personality, but they fail to convey that God is Be-ing. Women now who are experiencing the shock of nonbeing and the surge of self-affirmation against this are inclined to perceive transcendence as the Verb in which we participate—live, move, and have our being.

Thank You, Lord (excerpt)
Maya Angelou

I see You
Brown-skinned,
Neat Afro,
Full lips,
A little goatee.
A Malcolm,
Martin,
Du Bois.
Sunday services become sweeter when you're
    Black,
Then I don't have to explain why
I was out balling the town down,
Saturday night.

Thank you, Lord.
I want to thank You, Lord
For life and all that's in it.
Thank You for the day
And for the hour and for the minute.
I know many are gone,
I'm still living on,
I want to thank You.

Sexism and God-Talk (excerpt)
Rosemary Ruether

God/ess liberates us from this false and alienated world, not by an endless continuation of the same trajectory of alienation but as a constant breakthrough that points us to new possibilities that are, at the same time, the regrounding of ourselves in the primordial matrix, the original harmony. The liberating encounter with God/ess is always an encounter with our authentic selves resurrected from underneath the alienated self. It is not experienced against, but in and through relationships, healing our broken relations with our bodies, with other people, with nature. We have no adequate name for the true God/ess, the "I am who I shall become." Intimations of Her/His name will appear as we emerge from false naming of God/ess modeled on patriarchal alienation.

Apotheosis of the Kitchen Goddess II
Teresa Noelle Roberts

There is a goddess and I know her. Her hands are not clean,
And she is large and strong and not too young. She wears
A sweatshirt with a hood and jeans, and sells black-purple
Eggplant, spinach, bright broccoli, sixty cents
The pound at the Greenmarket at Union Square. Her slat-side truck
Has Pennsylvania plates, and she says she lives near Lancaster.
But I know the truth, because her calloused hands turn earth
To things good to eat, and green, and lovely.

They say she is veiled
Judy Grahn

They say she is veiled
and a mystery. That is
one way of looking.
Another
is that she is where
she always has been,
exactly in place,
and it is we,
we who are mystified,
we who are veiled
and without faces.

When the Saints Come Marching In
Audre Lorde

Plentiful sacrifice and believers in redemption
are all that is needed
so any day now
I expect some new religion
to rise up like tear gas

from the streets of New York
erupting like a rank pavement smell
released by the garbage-trucks'
baptismal drizzle.

The high priests have been ready and waiting
with their incense pans full of fire.
I do not know the rituals
the exhaltations
nor what name of the god
the survivors will worship
I only know she will be terrible
and very busy
and very old.

October (excerpt)
Audre Lorde

Seboulisa, mother of power
keeper of birds
fat and beautiful
give me the strength of your eyes
to remember
what I have learned
help me to attend with passion
these tasks at my hand for doing.

Carry my heart to some shore
that my feet will not shatter
do not let me pass away
before I have a name
for this tree
under which I am lying.
Do not let me die
still
needing to be stranger.

The Spiral Dance (excerpt)
Starhawk

The importance of the Goddess symbol for women cannot be overstressed. The image of the Goddess inspires women to see ourselves as divine, our bodies as sacred, the changing phases of our lives as holy, our aggression as healthy, our anger as purifying, and our power to nurture and create, but also to limit and destroy when necessary, as the very force that sustains all life. Through the Goddess, we can discover our strength, enlighten our minds, own our bodies, and celebrate our emotions. We can move beyond narrow, constricting roles and become whole.

The Goddess is also important for men. The oppression of men in Father God-ruled patriarchy is perhaps less obvious but no less tragic than that of women. Men are encouraged to identify with a model no human being can successfully emulate: to be minirulers of narrow universes. They are internally split, into a "spiritual" self that is supposed to conquer their baser animal and emotional natures. They are at war with themselves: in the West, to "conquer" sin; in the East, to "conquer" desire or ego. Few escape from these wars undamaged.

Nothing So Wise
Jeanne Lohmann

There is nothing so wise as a circle.
Rilke

The arc of an egg
bends hands
to shape prayer,

the shell
unbroken,
the heavy yolk
floating.

Our fingers
curving always
inward, become a cup,
an open bowl.

Prayer is
circumference
we may not
reach around,

space for all we cannot hold,
the rim of Love toward which we lean.

Meditations with Julian of Norwich (excerpt)
Julian of Norwich

God wants to be thought of
as our Lover.
I must see myself so bound in love
as if everything that has been done
has been done for me.
That is to say,
the Love of God makes such a unity
in us
that when we see this unity
no one is able to separate oneself
from another.

Inventing Sin
George Ella Lyon

God signs to us
    we cannot read
She shouts
    we take cover
She shrugs
    and trains leave
        the tracks

Our schedules! we moan
Our loved ones

God is fed up
All the oceans she gave us
All the fields
All the acres of steep seedful forests
And we did what
    Invented the Great Chain
        of Being and
      the chain saw
    Invented sin

God sees us now
    gorging ourselves &
    starving our neighbors
    starving ourselves &
    storing our grain
& She says

I've had it
    you cast your trash
    upon the waters—
    it's rolling in

    You stuck your fine fine finger
    into the mystery of life
        to find death

    & you did
    you learned how to end
    the world
    in nothing flat

Now you come crying
    to your mommy
Send us a miracle
Prove that you exist

Look at your hand, I say
Listen to your scared heart
Do you have to haul the tide in
sweeten the berries on the vine

I set you down
a miracle among miracles
You want more
It's your turn
You show me

Teeth

Susan Griffin

She who usually feeds us
is in a bad mood.
Are you trying to eat me up?
she shouts.
She bares her teeth
and makes a low noise.
With a disgusted gesture
she tells us
Go study your manners.
And wipe your feet,
she adds.

Not So. Not So.

Anne Sexton

I cannot walk an inch
without trying to walk to God.
I cannot move a finger
without trying to touch God.
Perhaps it is this way:
He is in the graves of the horses.
He is in the swarm, the frenzy of the bees.
He is in the tailor mending my pantsuit.
He is in Boston, raised up by the skyscrapers.
He is in the bird, that shameless flyer.
He is in the potter who makes clay into a kiss.

Heaven replies:
Not so! Not so!

I say thus and thus
and heaven smashes my words.

Is not God in the hiss of the river?

Not so! Not so!

Is not God in the ant heap,
stepping, clutching, dying, being born?

Not so! Not so!

Where then?
I cannot move an inch.

Look to your heart
that flutters in and out like a moth.
God is not indifferent to your need.
You have a thousand prayers
but God has one.

Woman's Call to the Ministry (excerpt)
Caroline Julia Bartlett

I believe that the greatest need of the church is to be *mothered*. Until the creeds are humanized, which were formulated by the early "church fathers" and by our Puritan forefathers; until the lost balance of religion is restored by the restoration of the *woman* element to the mutilated human and the mutilated divine; until the motherhood as well as the fatherhood of God is recognized by this world of self-made half-orphans; until these things be, the supreme call to the ministry that vibrates through the world to-day is to womanhood to give herself to the service of unifying and uplifting humanity, and bringing it up to the true knowledge and glad service of our Father and Mother God.

Nape

Jan Epton Seale

Here's praise to the nape of the neck,
a much neglected organ. Become a nape watcher

and you see strawberries stamped
at the turnstile of birth; an overhang of hair—

natural queue, leftover of the widow's peak,
or tail of a valentine, which leads me to say

the nape of the neck is a touch key of love:
feather-stroked, the whole board lights up.

The hair at the nape stays young forever.
Ancients go to their graves black-naped,

which leads me to say: when I die,
I'd rather not be redeemed like a gymnast recovering

on a trampoline, springing from grave
to feet blinded by an eastern sun. Rather

let God come like a thick dumb mother cat,
pick up what's left by the nape of its neck,

and move it to safe quarters.

Kali

Lucille Clifton

Kali
queen of fatality, she
determines the destiny
of things. nemesis.
the permanent guest
within ourselves.
woman of warfare,

of the chase, bitch
of blood sacrifice and death.
dread mother. the mystery
ever present in us and
outside us. the
terrible hindu woman God
Kali.
who is black.

Our Passion for Justice (excerpt)
Carter Heyward

We touch this strength, our power, who we are in the world, when we are
most fully in touch with one another and with the world. There is no doubt in
my mind that, in so doing, we are participants in ongoing incarnation, bringing god to life in the world. For god is nothing other than the eternally creative source of our relational power, our common strength, a god whose movement is to empower, bringing us into our own together, a god whose name in
history is love. . . .

In This Motherless Geography
Elaine Orr

As a child
I knew everything.
The spaces between
my fingers, the
third and fourth stanzas
of hymns, the underbellies
of old furniture.

When I was married,
I knew less, but
still something.

Now, like Dante,
at the middle of my life,
I know almost nothing.
I have forgotten
the shapes of stars
and even the hands
of my son.

I know only the bright hunger
in my belly,
centered and true
as a child's question; it leads
me on in this motherless geography.
If History calls me
I may return, but not

As I was. This time
I will not so easily
throw away my good name.
I will withhold my self
from the offering plate.
Prayers will be said
for my own homecoming.
And I will bend
like bamboo in the wind
but never break, knowing
that I and God are One,
that I am not
Forsaken.
And our soprano
voices will twine like sturdy rope,
and Our Stories will be written
in the blood of our own births.

for colored girls who have considered suicide when the rainbow is enuf (excerpt)
Ntozake Shange

i sat up one nite walkin a boardin house
screamin/ cryin/ the ghost of another woman
who waz missin what i waz missin
i wanted to jump up outta my bones
& be done wit myself
leave me alone
& go on in the wind
it waz too much
i fell into a numbness
til the only tree i cd see
took me up in her branches
held me in the breeze
made me dawn dew
that chill at daybreak
the sun wrapped me up swingin rose light everywhere
the sky laid over me like a million men
i waz cold/ i waz burnin up/ a child
& endlessly weavin garments for the moon
wit my tears

i found god in myself
& i loved her/ i loved her fiercely

Meditations with Hildegard of Bingen (excerpt)
Hildegard of Bingen

I am the one whose praise
echoes on high.

I adorn all the earth.

I am the breeze
that nurtures all things
green.
I encourage blossoms to flourish with ripening fruits.

I am led by the spirit to feed
the purest streams.

I am the rain
coming from the dew
that causes the grasses to laugh
with the joy of life.

I call forth tears,
the aroma of holy work.

I am the yearning for good.

Resurrection
Margaret Atwood

I see now I see
now I cannot see

earth is a blizzard in my eyes

I hear now

        the rustle of the snow

the angels listening above me

        thistles bright with sleet
        gathering

waiting for the time
to reach me
up to the pillared
sun, the final city

        or living towers

unrisen yet
whose dormant stones lie folding
their holy fire around me

(but the land shifts with frost
and those who have become the stone
voices of the land
shift also to say

god is not
the voice in the whirlwind

god is the whirlwind

at the last
judgement we will all be trees

Holy the Firm (excerpt)
Annie Dillard

Every day is a god, each day is a god, and holiness holds forth in time. I worship each god, I praise each day splintered down, splintered down and wrapped in time like a husk, a husk of many colors spreading, at dawn fast over the mountains split.

I wake in a god. I wake in arms holding my quilt, holding me as best they can inside my quilt.

Someone is kissing me—already. I wake, I cry "Oh," I rise from the pillow. Why should I open my eyes?

I open my eyes. The god lifts from the water. His head fills the bay. He is Puget Sound, the Pacific; his breast rises from pastures; his fingers are firs; islands slide wet down his shoulders. Islands slip blue from his shoulders and glide over the water, the empty, lighted water like a stage.

Today's god rises, his long eyes flecked in clouds. He flings his arms, spreading colors; he arches, cupping sky in his belly; he vaults, vaulting and spread, holding all and spread on me like skin.

Teaching a Stone to Talk (excerpt)
Annie Dillard

At a certain point you say to the woods, to the sea, to the mountains, the world, Now I am ready. Now I will stop and be wholly attentive. You empty yourself and wait, listening. After a time you hear it: there is nothing there. There is nothing but those things only, those created objects, discrete, growing or holding, or swaying, being rained on or raining, held, flooding or ebbing, standing, or spread. You feel the world's word as a tension, a hum, a single chorused note everywhere the same. This is it: this hum is the silence. . . .

*

The silence is all there is. It is the alpha and the omega. It is God's brooding over the face of the waters; it is the blended note of the ten thousand things, the whine of wings. You take a step in the right direction to pray to this silence, and even to address the prayer to "World." Distinctions blur. Quit your tents. Pray without ceasing.

Epiphany
Pem Kremer

Lynn Schmidt says
  she saw You once as prairie grass,
  Nebraska prairie grass;

  she climbed out of her car on a hot highway,
  leaned her butt on the nose of her car,
  looked out over one great flowing field,
  stretching beyond her sight until the horizon came:
  vastness, she says,
  responsive to the *slightest shift* of wind,
          full of infinite change,
          all One.

She says when she can't pray
She calls up Prairie Grass.

The Measure of My Days (excerpt)
Florida Scott-Maxwell

Life is a tragic mystery. We are pierced and driven by laws we only half understand, we find that the lesson we learn again and again is that of accepting heroic helplessness. Some uncomprehended law holds us at a point of contradiction where we have no choice, where we do not like that which we love, where good and bad are inseparable partners impossible to tell apart, and where we—heart-broken and ecstatic, can only resolve the conflict by blindly taking it into our hearts. This used to be called being in the hands of God. Has anyone any better words to describe it?

Eli, Eli
Miriam Kessler

My God, My God, he cried,
if he is quoted right. . . .
Somehow that moan is comforting
to us, alone at night,
who tremble, daring dawn,
that He, so wise and strong,
should weep and ask for aid.
Somehow, my lovely distant god,
it makes me less afraid.

The Color Purple (excerpt)
Alice Walker

Here's the thing, say Shug. The thing I believe. God is inside you and inside everybody else. You come into the world with God. But only them that search for it inside find it. And sometimes it just manifest itself even if you not looking, or don't know what you looking for. Trouble do it for most folks, I think. Sorrow, lord. Feeling like shit.

It? I ast.

Yeah, It. God ain't a he or a she, but a It.

But what do it look like? I ast.

Don't look like nothing, she say. It ain't a picture show. It ain't something you can look at apart from anything else, including yourself. I believe God is everything, say Shug. Everything that is or ever was or ever will be. And when you can feel that, and be happy to feel that, you've found It.

Shug a beautiful something, let me tell you. She frown a little, look out cross the yard, lean back in her chair, look like a big rose.

She say, My first step from the old white man was trees. Then air. Then birds. The other people. But one day when I was sitting quiet and feeling like a motherless child, which I was, it come to me: that feeling of being part of everything, not separate at all. I knew that if I cut a tree, my arm would bleed. And I laughed and cried and I run all around the house. I knew just what it was. In fact, when it happen, you can't miss it. It sort of like you know what, she say, grinning and rubbing high up on my thigh.

Shug! I say.

Oh, she say. God love all them feelings. That's some of the best stuff God did. And when you know God loves 'em you enjoys 'em a lot more. You can just relax, go with everything that's going, and praise God by liking what you like.

God don't think it dirty? I ast.

Naw, she say. God made it. Listen, God love everything you love—and a mess of stuff you don't. But more than anything else, God love admiration.

You saying God vain? I ast.

Naw, she say. Not vain, just wanting to share a good thing. I think it pisses God off if you walk by the color purple in a field somewhere and don't notice it.

Mass for the Day of St. Thomas Didymus (excerpt)
Denise Levertov

God then,
encompassing all things, is
defenseless? Omnipotence
has been tossed away, reduced
to a wisp of damp wool?

And we,
frightened, bored, wanting
only to sleep till catastrophe
has raged, clashed, seethed and gone by without us,
wanting then
to awaken in quietude without remembrance of agony,

we who in shamefaced private hope
had looked to be plucked from fire and given
a bliss we deserved for having imagined it,

is it implied that *we*
must protect this perversely weak
animal, whose muzzle's nudgings
suppose there is milk to be found in us?
Must hold to our icy hearts
a shivering God?

So be it.
Come, rag of pungent
quiverings,
dim star.
Let's try
if something human still
can shield you,
spark
of remote light.

The Thread

Denise Levertov

Something is very gently,
invisibly, silently,
pulling at me—a thread
or net of threads
finer than cobweb and as
elastic. I haven't tried
the strength of it. No barbed hook
pierced and tore me. Was it
not long ago this thread
began to draw me? Or
way back? Was I
born with its knot about my
neck, a bridle? Not fear
but a stirring
of wonder makes me
catch my breath when I feel
the tug of it when I thought
it had loosened itself and gone.

The Task

Denise Levertov

As if God were an old man
always upstairs, sitting about
in sleeveless undershirt, asleep,
arms folded, stomach rumbling,
his breath from open mouth
strident, presaging death . . .

No, God's in the wilderness next door
—that huge tundra room, no walls and a sky roof—
busy at the loom. Among the berry bushes,
rain or shine, that loud clacking and whirring,
irregular but continuous;
God is absorbed in work, and hears
the spacious hum of bees, not the din,
and hears far-off
our screams. Perhaps
listens for prayers in that wild solitude.
And hurries on with the weaving:
till it's done, the great garment woven,
our voices, clear under the familiar
    blocked-out clamor of the task,
can't stop their
               terrible beseeching. God
imagines it sifting through, at last, to music
in the astounded quietness, the loom idle,
the weaver at rest.

Re-Mything

More surely than anything else, we are defined by our stories—the cultural myths we hear from our earliest days. In Western culture woman has been defined from the perspective of the dominant male. She is helpless, until a man comes to save her (Snow White). She is known by only her husband's name, for she has no identity apart from her relationship to him (Lot's wife, Job's wife). She is not the artist herself, but rather the inspiration to the male artist (the Muse). Women are now revising these myths in order to expose the hidden and terribly destructive messages inherent in them. Only as old patterns in our consciousness crumble are new patterns possible. Let us take a hard look at the canonized mythology that has kept us from spiritual wholeness. Let us tell our own untold stories.

The Tree
Cinda Thompson

Do you know
of loneliness
When the burden of apples is
so great, the branches split
And red drips into green grass
in Eden
There was no serpent
though Adam
Pushed my body away
helpmeet once
Witness to a husband's sleeping
I know all
Children, Cain and Abel alike
come to
My breast and I am punished
for knowledge
Of disease or discovery
of soft sucking mouths and
Pain threatens to shackle
legs to earth,
But my belly swells, the moon rises
genesis-full
Cursed, he swore, I say
I am
Eve. Be aware. I am
your mother.

The Sacrifice
Chana Bloch

1

In wings and starched
white gowns, the angels crowd
all on one bench, wingtips
rustling for room.

Sarah's pantry is bare.
Abraham stoops (no wings) before
the splendor of guests.

The angels look at him, laughing.
They have time.

2
The patriarch in black takes
candle and knife
like cutlery,
rehearsing under his breath
the Benediction
on the Death of an Only Son.

Isaac stoops under the raw wood,
carries his father on his back,
candle, velvet and all.

3
On the woodpile
Isaac's body waits
as women wait,
fever trilling under his skin.

He will remember the blade's
white silence,
a lifetime
under his father's eyes.

Ruth

Diane Q. Lewis

1
Her God began to pulse through me
leaving me filled with passion
for sky and hills. Though Naomi
had grown bitter with the death
of her husband and sons
I felt a kinship with her.

When she spoke of returning
home I knew that I must go too, must
leave this land begun when father and daughter
shared the same bed, seek the God
who did not claim children as offerings.

She rode the donkey loaded with most
of our possessions. I carried the rest.
In the evening as her hands soothed
my shoulders and back she repeated the story
of her people dispossessed in the wilderness.
Sometimes at night, frightened
awake by the shriek of a hyrax,
I would remember that Naomi said
all creatures were created
good. Peace would surround me. Those
mornings I arose restored.

At the Jordan when I bathed my skin
burned the color of almond bark I buried
the veil and amulet of Chemosh.

Naomi's God was mine now;
we were bound, one desire, one soul.

2

In the fields where I gleaned barley
the women reviled me, called me
harlot, and turned away; men eyed me
with the same lust that men in Moab had.
I kept my head low as I labored.

On mornings when my body suffered rising
so tired was I from the day before
Naomi strengthened me with stories
of Deborah and Sarah, Rachel and Leah.

There was one man, Boaz, our kinsman
who owned the land. As he strode
over the gleaming fields and spoke
to his workers I knew the power of spirit
moved through him like the unseen power
that causes the eagle to soar.
He stood before me and said

—Lift up your head and tell me who you are.
—I am Ruth, your kinswoman.
—Come, and eat with me.
And he put before me
bread dipped in wine, and goat cheese.
I was grateful and bowed my face to the ground.
From that time on his spirit
caused no man to touch me.

As the sun brightened the fields I bent
again and again. Each day my baskets overflowed.
I was exalted by my God.

As the candle flame, as the fire, I am light.
As the sun. I am light, I am light.

    3
On the night of the winnowing when Naomi
told me to wash and go to Boaz while he
slept I did as she bid. I smoothed
my skin with aloes and dressed carefully.
I lay quietly at his feet as she had
instructed me and watched the moon
rise until it illumined his face.
Thereupon he awoke.

He accepted me as his and I
rested in his care throughout the night.
In the first light he blessed me saying,
—Open your cloak
that has been washed of doubt
and I will fill it with love.

As the tree rooted in earth, I am home.
As the stars in the night sky, I am home, I am home.

Lot's Wife

Cherra S. Ransom

The advice was good—not to look back—
But was wasted on the woman, water in a sieve.
She had spent a lifetime looking backward,
Remembering the towers of Ur, unhallowed yet familiar,
The children withering on the march,
Their graves milestones along the way,
The sinister new city like some exotic rotting fruit,
A strange shrill tongue, the hard faces watching,
New ways hardening into habit
Like wounds puckering into scars.
She remembered, but was numb, silent behind her veil,
Until the sudden flight.

Now stumbling from Sodom to still another exile,
It was not fear that stopped her in the end.
It was all those unshed tears that choked her veins
And hardened round her heart.
Pausing and turning and looking homeward,
She could not see the burning plain between.
The slow precipitate of years
Crystallized behind her eyes.
Her sight blurred. Her feet were stone.
She stood an instant carved in salt,
A monument that fell
Before the cities sank upon the smoking earth.

Job's Wife (excerpt)

Betsy Sholl

Then his wife said to him, "Do you still hold fast your integrity?
Curse God and die."
—Job 2 : 9

Yes, I said it.
And I told him to pull out his hair,
scream till his eyes turned black.

Some integrity,
scraping himself with broken pots.
An expert on God.
I'm an expert on mustard plaster,
bad breath.

On ten children—
their shoulders, their eyes,
the curve of their buttocks
I knew better than my own hands.

So you're God.
Tell me I'm straw, chaff, mist.

Tell me the sea has springs
deep and cold as dreams
that make me wake exhausted.

Enough thunder.
What have you done
with my children?

Poem for Flora
Nikki Giovanni

when she was little
and colored and ugly with short
straightened hair
and a very pretty smile
she went to sunday school to hear
'bout nebuchadnezzar the king
of the jews

and she would listen

shadrach, meshach and abednego in the fire

and she would learn

how god was neither north
nor south east or west
with no color but all
she remembered was that
Sheba was Black and comely

and she would think

i want to be
like that

Delilah

Ellen Bryant Voigt

It wasn't the money or their silly
political speeches. I planned it
long before they came to mince
and whimper into their spit-stained
beards. What would they know
of power? Such thin sticks for my
magnificent boar, swinging a jaw-bone,
smashing and driving—ah, Samson!
your loins' heat, the sweet weight
of your thighs. . . . That I could tame,
outwit, be stronger than *that*, I teased
the secret out. And in the early
morning, while the Philistines
leered from the fringed curtain,
while the royal harlots swayed
in their tents like frail-stemmed
flowers, while laborious wives molded
the meal-cake, their bellies warped
with children and children clutching
their slack breasts—in that hour
of last darkness, dressed in satin
split to an oiled thigh, I drove
my whetted shears to your sprawled
heap and the manly seat of power.

Abishag
Shirley Kaufman

. . . and let her lie in thy bosom that the lord my king may get heat.
—1 Kings 1:2

That's what they ordered
for the old man
to dangle around his neck,
send currents of fever
through his phlegmatic nerves, something
like rabbit fur, silky,
or maybe a goat-hair blanket
to tickle his chin.

He can do nothing else
but wear her, pluck at her body
like a lost bird
pecking in winter.
He spreads her out
like a road map, trying
to find his way from one point
to another, unable.

She thinks if she pinches
his hand it will turn to powder.
She feels his thin claws, his wings
spread over her like arms, not bones
but feathers ready to fall.
She suffers the jerk
of his feeble legs. Take it easy,
she tells him, cruelly
submissive in her bright flesh.
He's cold from the fear
of death, the sorrow
of failure, night after night
he shivers with her breasts
against him like an accusation
her mouth slightly open,
her hair spilling everywhere.

Lucille Clifton

the dead shall rise again
whoever say
dust must be dust
don't see the trees
smell rain
remember africa
everything that goes
can come
stand up
even the dead shall rise

mary
Lucille Clifton

this kiss
as soft as cotton

over my breasts
all shiny bright

something is in this night
oh Lord have mercy on me

i feel a garden
in my mouth

between my legs
i see a tree

holy night
Lucille Clifton

joseph, i afraid of stars,
their brilliant seeing.
so many eyes. such light.
joseph, i cannot still these limbs,
i hands keep moving toward i breasts,
so many stars. so bright.
joseph, is wind burning from east
joseph, i shine, oh joseph,   oh
illuminated night.

Jesus Dies
Anne Sexton

From up here in the crow's nest
I see a small crowd gather.
Why do you gather, my townsmen?
There is no news here.
I am not a trapeze artist.
I am busy with My dying.
Three heads lolling,
bobbing like bladders.
No news.
The soldiers down below
laughing as soldiers have done for centuries.
No news.
We are the same men,
you and I,
the same sort of nostrils,
the same sort of feet.
My bones are oiled with blood
and so are yours.
My heart pumps like a jack rabbit in a trap
and so does yours.
I want to kiss God on His nose and watch Him sneeze
and so do you.
Not out of disrespect.
Out of pique.
Out of a man-to-man thing.

I want heaven to descend and sit on My dinner plate
and so do you.
I want God to put His steaming arms around Me
and so do you.
Because we need.
Because we are sore creatures.
My townsmen,
go home now.
I will do nothing extraordinary.
I will not divide in two.
I will not pick out My white eyes.
Go now,
this is a personal matter,
a private affair and God knows
none of your business.

The Feast of the Assumption of the Virgin
Ellen Bryant Voigt

Matins

Felix rapina. The flap
and whistle of the angel's
wings, the public birth,
the chastened motherhood.
When they led her from her son's
cruel scaffolding, she wanted
no more miracles. Now this.
Plucked up to heaven, a pressed
flower—her body is used
for a million statuary.

Nones

The church sweats in its dark stone.
The triptych, a pamphlet of roses,
flanks the altar. In one stained
panel of window, Joseph provides detail.
The Madonna mourns from a nearby table;
one hand is raised
as if reaching for fruit. Among
the murmuring candles, a solicitor
spews his secret into her ear.

Mary,
Holy Vessel, Queen of the Martyrs:
in the mountains of Zakopane

the rutted street swells
with women, bringing you flowers.
See how they cradle

the passionate blossoms. Precious
Mother, the village is blooming. Here,
in a row by the plain wood houses,

here, by the roadside,
the young girls are gathered.
Each wears white lace, hand-made

for marriage; each
is chosen, blessed by the father;
and when the bells release

a shower of pollen,
each mouth opens to rapture
like a wound.

to joan
Lucille Clifton

joan
did you never hear
in the soft rushes of france
merely the whisper of french grass
rubbing against leathern
sounding now like a windsong
now like a man?
did you never wonder
oh fantastical joan,
did you never cry in the sun's face
unreal   unreal? did you never run
villageward
hands pushed out toward your apron?

and just as you knew that your mystery
was broken for all time
did they not fall then
soft as always
into your ear
calling themselves michael
among beloved others?
and you
sister   sister
did you not then sigh
my voices   my voices   of course?

Riding Hood
Betsy Sholl

My daughter makes songs from the words
she hears, mixing *august barley grief*
into a broth sloshing inside its jar.

There's no wolf in her skipping
red-shirted song.
Where did I learn to fear?

Surely I am happy
hearing her beside me
singing as I used to sing
in the back seat of the car
serenading the black trees
at the edge of the road
as the bald astonished moon
flew out of the branches.

We walk down the street gathering leaves.
What stirs the trees? One of my mother's
long sighs, one of her words meaning *loss*,
that squint in her eyes looking at all
that might gobble us up.

But, Mother, I wasn't eaten.
Poor though we were, the dog didn't snarl.

Grandmother lived next door.
I never entered a stranger's car.

For all your worry,
don't you think you were a fine woman
for me to study, to learn by heart?

August august barley grief
and blessings flow. My daughter sings
on and on. *My mommy my mommy*
my mom-mee-mom. Why should I grieve?

We sit on the steps humming.
The moon rises through the trees, lips pursed
in the first quizzical O of a song.
So what if death cruises the block
in his shiny car leaning out the window
calling to her—My daughter
shake your yellow hair at him.

I and Thou
Chana Bloch

1
How I hate you tonight!
I tick off
the bumps on your back,
your hangnails, the acid
smell of your sweat.
You corrode my skin.
Who let you in?
When did you grow that nose?
You changed your name.
Of course you're to blame.
What do you care?
You don't know me,
you don't know me.

2
For your information, my toes
are rosebuds
of superior breeding.

Yours are tough,
discolored,
misshapen by shoes.

And how did you ever get
tobacco stains
on the bottoms of your feet?

3

The princess
picked up the Little Green Frog
spotted ugh! all over
and threw it just as
hard as she could
against the castle wall.

"Here's your chance!"
she cried.
"Now become
a prince."

The Two Gretels

Robin Morgan

The two Gretels were exploring the forest.
Hansel was home,
sending up flares.

Sometimes one Gretel got afraid.
She said to the other Gretel,
"I think I'm afraid."
"Of course we are," Gretel replied.

Sometimes the other Gretel whispered,
with a shiver,
"You think we should turn back?"
To which her sister Gretel answered,
"We can't. We forgot the breadcrumbs."

So, they went forward
because
they simply couldn't imagine the way back.

And eventually, they found the Gingerbread House,
and the Witch, who was really, they discovered,
the Great Good Mother Goddess,
and they all lived happily ever after.

The Moral of this story is:

Those who would have the whole loaf,
let alone the House,
had better throw away their breadcrumbs.

Myth
Muriel Rukeyser

Long afterward, Oedipus, old and blinded, walked the
roads.   He smelled a familiar smell.   It was
the Sphinx.   Oedipus said, "I want to ask one question.
Why didn't I recognize my mother?"   "You gave the
wrong answer," said the Sphinx.   "But that was what
made everything possible," said Oedipus.   "No," she said.
"When I asked, What walks on four legs in the morning,
two at noon, and three in the evening, you answered,
Man.   You didn't say anything about woman."
"When you say Man," said Oedipus, "you include women
too. Everyone knows that."   She said, "That's what
you think."

Maxim
Josephine Miles

It is said that certain orientational concepts of
        an ontological sort
Such as despair, sin, salvation, loneliness
Derive a certain richness from experience.

I noticed today at the Rose Bowl Parade
In the Romeo and Juliet float representing Wonder Bread,
How lonely romeo shirtsleeved

In the frosty morning air looked, saluting
(1) the balcony made of thousands of blossoms of
    pink winter stock,
And (2) the curbstone crowd.

This won the sweepstakes prize, yet Juliet
Smiled in despair in the frosty morning air,
Receiving her certain richness from experience.

The Mermaid
Lisel Mueller

All day he had felt her stirring
under the boat, and several times
when the net had tightened, frog-nervous,
he had bungled the pulling-in,
half-glad of the stupid, open mouths
he could throw back.
           At sundown
the shifting and holding of time and air
had brought her to the still surface,
to sun herself in the last, slow light
where lilies and leeches tangled and rocked.
He could have taken her then, aimed his net
as dragonfly hunters do when the glassy gliding
of rainbows goes to their heads,
could have carried her home on tiptoe
and lifted her lightly, ever so lightly,
over his sill.
           And, hopeless, knew
that to have her alive was only this:
the sounding, casting, waiting, seeing
and praying the light not to move,
not yet to round the bay of her shoulder
and passing, release her
to the darkness he would not enter.

ego-tripping (there may be a reason why)
Nikki Giovanni

I was born in the congo
I walked to the fertile crescent and built
    the sphinx
I designed a pyramid so tough that a star
      that only glows every one hundred years falls
      into the center giving divine perfect light
I am bad

I sat on the throne
    drinking nectar with allah
I got hot and sent an ice age to europe
    to cool my thirst
My oldest daughter is nefertiti
    the tears from my birth pains
    created the nile
I am a beautiful woman

I gazed on the forest and burned
    out the sahara desert
    with a packet of goat's meat
    and a change of clothes
I crossed it in two hours
I am a gazelle so swift
    so swift you can't catch me

    For a birthday present when he was three
I gave my son hannibal an elephant
    He gave me rome for mother's day
My strength flows ever on

My son noah built new/ark and
I stood proudly at the helm
    as we sailed on a soft summer day

I turned myself into myself and was
    jesus
    men intone my loving name

    All praises All praises
I am the one who would save

0

I sowed diamonds in my back yard
My bowels deliver uranium
    the filings from my fingernails are
    semi-precious jewels
    On a trip north
I caught a cold and blew
My nose giving oil to the arab world
I am so hip even my errors are correct
I sailed west to reach east and had to round off
    the earth as I went
    The hair from my head thinned and gold was
    laid across three continents

I am so perfect so divine so ethereal so surreal
I cannot be comprehended
    except by my permission

I mean . . . I . . . can fly
    like a bird in the sky . . .

Everywoman Her Own Theology
Alicia Ostriker

I am nailing them up to the cathedral door
Like Martin Luther. Actually, no,
I don't want to resemble that *Schmutzkopf*
(See Erik Erikson and N. O. Brown
On the Reformer's anal aberrations,
Not to mention his hatred of Jews and peasants),
So I am thumbtacking these ninety-five
Theses to the bulletin board in my kitchen.

My proposals, or should I say requirements,
Include at least one image of a god,
Virile, beard optional, one of a goddess,
Nubile, breast size approximating mine,
One divine baby, one lion, one lamb,
All nude as figs, all dancing wildly,
All shining. Reproducible
In marble, metal, in fact any material.

Ethically, I am looking for
An absolute endorsement of loving-kindness.
No loopholes except maybe mosquitoes.
Virtue and sin will henceforth be discouraged,
Along with suffering and martyrdom.
There will be no concept of infidels;
Consequently the faithful must entertain
Themselves some other way than killing infidels.

And so forth and so on. I understand
This piece of paper is going to be
Spattered with wine one night at a party
And covered over with newer pieces of paper.
That is how it goes with bulletin boards.
Nevertheless it will be there.
Like an invitation, like a chalk pentangle,
It will emanate certain occult vibrations.

If something sacred wants to swoop from the universe
Through a ceiling, and materialize,
Folding its silver wings,
In a kitchen, and bump its chest against mine,
My paper will tell this being where to find me.

The Word

"In the beginning was the Word." The first chapter of John announces the incarnational principle of language. It is not easy for women to write. We have been afforded neither time nor space within the traditional demands of our role, and we have not been taken seriously as writers when we have chosen to go that hard route in spite of cultural restraints. But we are called upon to bear witness. The following selections speak of the power of language in speaking the truth, in building community, in giving courage. Naming carries weight and definition. Concepts shift. The new is born.

Why I Never Answered Your Letter
Nancy Willard

It's true I make books, but not often.
Mostly I am always feeding someone,
nine cats whose tails flag me down each morning
and who know a soft touch when they feel one,
and who write on my door in invisible milk:
Good for a handout. Good for a night's lodging.

Mostly I'm taking from Peter and not paying Paul.
My man comes home, dreaming of sirloin.
I ravage the house: three eggs and half a potato.
I embalm them in amorous spices with beautiful names.
It's true I make books, but mostly I make do.
The chapters of hunger are filled but nothing is finished.

At night a baby calls me for comfort and milk.
Someday I'll teach him to sing, to dance, and to draw,
to learn his letters, to speak like an honest man.
Right now I teach him to eat, and I tell him a story,
how an angel came to Saint John with a book in its hands,
saying, *Take and eat. It shall make thy belly bitter,*
but thou shalt know all people, all prophets, and all lands.

Words & Language: A Haggle (excerpt)
Paula Gunn Allen

There is an enormous difference between the way western people approach the use of language and the way tribal people approach it. [Tribal people] say the words are sacred. We don't mean that you are supposed to kneel down and worship them. We mean that you should in your being recognize that when you speak, your utterance has consequences inwardly and outwardly and that you are accountable for those consequences. You can't just say anything that comes to your head and then get distressed if another person acts on it. Now that other person may have misunderstood you, which means that they have a responsibility to find out exactly what you mean before they act, but the principle is still there. Without linguistic honor there can be no community, there can be no ethic, there can be no love, there can be no creative vision, there can be no peace, and there can be no relationship.

tell our daughters
Besmilr Brigham

each is beautiful
a woman's life
makes it (that awareness)
through her touch

    descendants
of strict age
set against vanity

not secure in loveliness

a girl is born
like a little bird opening its wing
she lifts her face
in a down of feathers

a rose
  opens its leaves
with such a natural care
that we give words for
petal deep
in the imagination

              a word becomes
              a bitter thing
              or a word is
              an imagination

tell our daughters   they are
fragile as a bird
strong as the rose
deep as a word

and let them make
their own growing time

             big with tenderness

Susan Griffin

One after another
our mother helps us to write
our little poems.
She says she likes them.
She says this is good you should
write down what I say.
She says *If it weren't for stories and poems*
if it weren't for stories and poems
but she never finishes this sentence.
She only raises her eyebrows.
And you, she says, you never finish
your sentence either, crying,
Mother, mother
give us
give us

"Naming" from Woman and Nature
Susan Griffin

Behind naming, beneath words, is something else. An existence named unnamed and unnameable. We give the grass a name, and earth a name. We say
grass and earth are separate. We know this because we can pull the grass free
of the earth and see its separate roots—but when the grass is free, it dies. We
say the inarticulate have no souls. We say the cow's eye has no existence outside ourselves, that the red wing of the blackbird has no thought, the roe of
the salmon no feeling, because we cannot name these. Yet for our own lives
we grieve all that cannot be spoken, that there is no name for, repeating for
ourselves the names of things which surround what cannot be named. We say
Heron and Loon, Coot and Killdeer, Snipe and Sandpiper, Gull and Hawk,
Eagle and Osprey, Pigeon and Dove, Oriole, Meadowlark, Sparrow. We say
Red Admiral and Painted Lady, Morning Cloak and Question Mark, Baltimore
and Checkerspot, Buckeye, Monarch, Viceroy, Mayfly, Stonefly, Cicada,
Leafhopper and Earwig, we say Sea Urchin and Sand Dollar, Starfish and
Sandworm. We say mucous membrane, uterus, cervix, ligament, vagina and
hymen, labia, orifice, artery, vessel, spine and heart. We say skin, blood,
breast, nipple, taste, nostril, green, eye, hair, we say vulva, hood, clitoris,

belly, foot, knee, elbow, pit, nail, thumb, we say tongue, teeth, toe, ear, we say ear and voice and touch and taste and we say again love, breast and beautiful and vulva, saying clitoris, saying belly, saying toes and soft, saying ear, saying ear, saying ear, ear and hood and hood and green and all that we say we are saying around that which cannot be said, cannot be spoken. But in a moment that which is behind naming makes itself known. Hand and breast know each one to the other. Wood in the table knows clay in the bowl. Air knows grass knows water knows mud knows beetle knows frost knows sunlight knows the shape of the earth knows death knows not dying. And all this knowledge is in the souls of everything, behind naming, before speaking, beneath words.

Poem for a Chorus
Marie Cartier

I am a woman with paper.
My lover's flesh, apricot silk, under my hand.
On the T.V., a special on Hiroshima.
 In nine seconds, 100,000 people killed.
Whose arms would I reach out to
in nine seconds?
Apricot silk ripples
How many hours do we spend apart?
 In Hiroshima people died in factories.
 Children at their desks.
 It was 8:11 a.m.
8:11 a.m. My lover at work.
I am at work.
A space between us—and then, nine seconds.
 An elderly Japanese gentleman weeps.
 He remembers a baby suckling a lifeless breast.
 "These hands turned the pages of a book,
 held a baby," he sees the mother's hands.
 "Her fingers curled into stumps,
 oozed a strange, grey liquid.
 The baby did not understand, and cried."
 He wipes his eyes carefully,
 "There were burns. Flesh ripped by wind.
 People impaled under parts of buildings.
 Politely asking for 'Some help. Please.   If you can.'

At the center, you see,
    it was really very quiet."
Yet, I am simply a woman with paper.
    my hand my home skin peach cream honeysuckle
I see their faces their arms and legs.
    sores running like split fruit
    their faces taut
They did not cry out.
At the center there was silence.
The significance I want to bring to my words
echoes strongest in the spaces between them.
Silence. Nine seconds.   Then silence.
    my lover's flesh peach silk
    torn back open mouthed silent screaming
What can I tell you, out there
beyond this small Colorado night?
    100,000 people killed in nine seconds, 1945.
    1987, a bomb 1,000 times more powerful,
    will leave 70 percent of the world's population—silent.
I tell you—I want us to live.
At the center there was silence.
    These hands turn the pages of books.
    Sit with paper and pen.
    I fold the paper into an airplane.
    Aim it towards a center of voices.
    Of voices.

A Way of Staying Sane (excerpt)
Maxine Kumin

I write these poems because I have to. I wrestle with my own notions of human depravity in this, and in other poems, not because I think the poem can change our foreign policy, soften the heart of the military-industrial complex that feeds on first-strike potential propaganda, or arouse the citizenry to acts of civil disobedience for peace, but because, for my own sanity (and yours, and yours), I must live the dream out to the end. It is important to act as if bearing witness matters. To write about the monstrous sense of alienation the poet feels in this culture of polarized hatreds is a way of staying sane. With the poem, I reach out to an audience equally at odds with official policy, and I celebrate our mutual humanness in an inhuman world.

The Last Class

Ellen Bryant Voigt

Put this in your notebooks:
All verse is occasional verse.
In March, trying to get home, distracted
and impatient at Gate 5 in the Greyhound station,
I saw a drunk man bothering a woman.
A poem depends on its detail
but the woman had her back to me,
and the man was just another drunk,
black in this case, familiar, dirty.
I moved past them both, got on the bus.

There is no further action to report.
The man is not a symbol. If what he said to her
touches us, we are touched by a narrative
we supply. What he said was, "I'm sorry,
I'm sorry," over and over, "I'm sorry,"
but you must understand he frightened the woman,
he meant to rob her of those few quiet
solitary moments sitting down,
waiting for the bus, before she headed home
and probably got supper for her family,
perhaps in a room in Framingham,
perhaps her child was sick.

My bus pulled out, made its usual turns
and parted the formal gardens from the Common,
both of them camouflaged by snow.
And as it threaded its way to open road,
leaving the city, leaving our sullen classroom,
I postponed my satchel of your poems
and wondered who I am to teach the young,
having come so far from honest love of the world;
I tried to recall how it felt
to live without grief; and then I wrote down
a few tentative lines about the drunk,
because of an old compulsion to record,
or sudden resolve not to be self-absorbed
and full of dread—
                    I wanted to salvage
something from my life, to fix
some truth beyond all change, the way

photographers of war, miles from the front,
lift print after print into the light,
each one further cropped and amplified,
pruning whatever baffles or obscures,
until the small figures are restored
as young men sleeping.

the making of poems
Lucille Clifton

the reason why i do it
though i fail and fail
in the giving of true names
is i am adam and his mother
and these failures are my job.

One Writer's Beginnings (excerpt)
Eudora Welty

I live in gratitude to my parents for initiating me—and as early as I begged for
it, without keeping me waiting—into knowledge of the word, into reading
and spelling, by way of the alphabet. They taught it to me at home in time for
me to begin to read before starting to school. I believe the alphabet is no
longer considered an essential piece of equipment for traveling through life.
In my day it was the keystone to knowledge. You learned the alphabet as you
learned to count to ten, as you learned "Now I lay me" and the Lord's Prayer
and your father's and mother's name and address and telephone number, all in
case you were lost.

My love for the alphabet, which endures, grew out of reciting it but,
before that, out of seeing the letters on the page. In my own story books,
before I could read them for myself, I fell in love with various winding, en-
chanted-looking initials drawn by Walter Crane at the heads of fairy tales. In
"Once upon a time," and "O" had a rabbit running it as a treadmill, his feet
upon flowers. When the day came, years later, for me to see the Book of
Kells, all the wizardry of letter, initial, and word swept over me a thousand
times over, and the illumination, the gold, seemed a part of the word's beauty
and holiness that had been there from the start.

Three Small Songs for the Muse
Kathleen Norris

1

My oldest friend looks for me
on a dark road.
Nights I can't sleep,
we are lonely together.

We are yellowjackets in late summer,
beating at the screen.
We are two old women holding hands
at the funeral of a friend.

We are two children playing
"Who Am I?"
You put your hands over my eyes
and in their darkness,
I know for sure
that at the end,
the playful stranger who appears
is not death
but love.

2

So you've come again
with a new face;
an unsettling thought
in my settled life.

You're a woman, a man.
You change the names for love
each time you come.

3

We walk in the ocean
not far from shore.
We walk on the bright shore
and you call me over
to show me something: a shell.
You name it, and we laugh.

We spend days talking,
doing very little.

For so long I'd been praying,
"Come to me."

"I'll find you," you said.
And you did.

A Visit

George Ella Lyon

I was securing the pin in the diaper
when someone banged on the door
and it was this guy
in an orange fishnet Florida Interstate
T-shirt
holding his bike helmet and saying

Hi, I'm the Muse.

You?

Yeah, name's Floyd.

Well, come on in. I'm in the middle
of a bunch of things.

Best place to begin. Now—

No. I mean I'm fixing dinner,
my little boy's awake, and—

Lady, Lady, Lady,
you'll never get off the fucking ground like that.
What're you cooking?

Millet.

God, the Lady eats like a bird.
Honey, you gotta have meat to make poems,
takes blood to make blood sing.

Be that as it may—

I can see you're not serious.
You got anything to drink?

Beer.

That'll do.

*

Here you go. You know
it came to me in the kitchen:
with you here, maybe I *could*
do some work. Dinner's ready for the oven,
my little boy's been changed.
Could you watch him awhile?

The *MUSE*?
The *MUSE* a fucking babysitter?
Who do you think you are?
I'm sacred, remember?
I'm holy shit—

Well, how are you going to help me
sucking on that bottle of beer?

Baby, I can take you to Bliss City
in one spin on my machine.
When I've finished, you'll be so inspired
your tits will blow up balloons.

Great. What about my son?

Ditch the kid awhile.
You can't fool around
wiping asses
when I'm ready to fly.

Fly? What about writing?
Remember words,
those heavy things—?

Jeez, she's climbing on her soapbox.
Go on then.   Who cares?
Scrape your life from mayonnaise jars.
You won't see me again.

Promise?

She and the Muse
Denise Levertov

Away he goes, the hour's delightful hero,
arrivederci: and his horse clatters
out of the courtyard, raising
a flurry of straw and scattering hens.

He turns in the saddle waving a plumed hat,
his saddlebags are filled with talismans,
mirrors, parchment histories, gifts and stones,
indecipherable clues to destiny.

He rides off in the dustcloud of his own
story, and when he has vanished she
who had stood firm to wave and watch
from the top step, goes in to the cool

flagstoned kitchen, clears honey and milk and bread
off the table, sweeps from the hearth
ashes of last night's fire, and climbs the stairs
to strip tumbled sheets from her wide bed.

              Now the long-desired
visit is over. The heroine
is a scribe. Returned to solitude,
eagerly she re-enters the third room,

the room hung with tapestries, scenes that change
whenever she looks away. Here is her lectern,
here her writing desk. She picks a quill,
dips it, begins to write. But not of him.

The Secret

Denise Levertov

Two girls discover
the secret of life
in a sudden line of
poetry.

I who don't know the
secret wrote
the line. They
told me

(through a third person)
they had found it
but not what it was,
not even

what line it was. No doubt
by now, more than a week
later, they have forgotten
the secret,

the line, the name of
the poem. I love them
for finding what
I can't find,

and for loving me
for the line I wrote:
and for forgetting it
so that

a thousand times, till death
finds them, they may
discover it again, in other
lines,

in other
happenings. And for
wanting to know it,
for

assuming there is
such a secret, yes,
for that
most of all.

'*I learned that her name was Proverb.*'
Denise Levertov

And the secret names
of all we meet who lead us deeper
into our labyrinth
of valleys and mountains, twisting valleys
and steeper mountains—
their hidden names are always,
like Proverb, promises:
Rune, Omen, Fable, Parable,
those we meet for only
one crucial moment, gaze to gaze,
or for years know and don't recognize

but of whom later a word
sings back to us
as if from high among leaves,
still near but beyond sight

drawing us from tree to tree
towards the time and the unknown place
where we shall know
what it is to arrive.

Credits

Allen   Excerpt from "Words and Language: A Haggle" by Paula Gunn Allen. Originally appeared in *Mama Bears News and Notes*, July 20, 1986. Copyright © by Paula Gunn Allen. Reprinted by permission of the author.

Alta   "3:1," excerpt from "7:3," excerpt from "2:7," excerpt from "3:6," "104," "29," and "Lorelei" from *The Shameless Hussy, Essays and Poetry by Alta* by Alta Gerry (Crossing Press). Copyright © by Alta Gerry. Reprinted by permission of the author.

Alvarez   "Ironing Their Clothes," "Greg's Got Custody of Sally," and "I Check My Parents' House" from *Homecoming* by Julia Alvarez. Copyright © 1984 by Julia Alvarez. Reprinted by permission of Grove Weidenfeld.

Angelou   "Elegy" from *Oh Pray My Wings Are Gonna Fit Me Well* by Maya Angelou. Copyright © 1975 by Maya Angelou. Reprinted by permission of Random House, Inc.

Angelou   Excerpt from "Thank you Lord" from *And Still I Rise* by Maya Angelou. Copyright © 1978 by Maya Angelou. Reprinted by permission of Random House, Inc.

Atwood   "Dream 2: Brian the Still-Hunter" and "Resurrection" from *The Journals of Susanna Moodie* by Margaret Atwood. Copyright © 1970 by Oxford University Press Canada. Reprinted by permission of Oxford University Press Canada.

Atwood   "It is dangerous to read newspapers" from *The Animals in That Country* by Margaret Atwood. Copyright © 1968 by Oxford University Press Canada. Reprinted by permission of Oxford University Press Canada.

Atwood   "Solstice Poem (v)" and "Five Poems for Grandmothers (iii)" from *Two-Headed Poems* by Margaret Atwood. Copyright © 1978 by Margaret Atwood. Reprinted by permission of Oxford University Press and Houghton Mifflin Company.

Baggett   "The Day Before They Bombed Nagasaki" by Rebecca Baggett originally appeared in *Poetry Flash*, December 1987. Copyright © by Rebecca Baggett. Reprinted by permission of the author.

Bass   "To praise" from *Early Ripening* by Ellen Bass. Originally published, in a different version, in *Calyx*, 1976. Copyright © by Ellen Bass. Reprinted by permission of the author.

Bateman   "Conspiracy," "Childhood of a Stranger," and "Beatitude" by Claire Bateman. Copyright © by Claire Bateman. Reprinted by permission of the author.

Becker   "The Gardner" by Robin Becker originally appeared in *Prairie Schooner*, Vol. 62, No. 2 (University of Nebraska Press, 1988). Reprinted by permission of the author.

Bloch   "Survivors" by Chana Bloch is reprinted from the *Graham House Review*. Copyright © by Chana Bloch. Reprinted by permission of the author.

Bloch   "White Petticoats" (formerly "Perfection") and "Rising to Meet It" by Chana Bloch are reprinted from *Poetry*. Copyright © by Chana Bloch. Reprinted by permission of the author.

Bloch   "Yom Kippur," "I and Thou," "The Sacrifice" and "Magnificat" are from *The Secrets of the Tribe* by Chana Bloch. Copyright © by Chana Bloch. Sheep Meadow Press, 1981. Reprinted by permission of the author.

Index

Abishag, 270
abortion, 103, 104, 105
Abraham and Isaac, 263–64
abundance, 33–34
abuse: child, 135–36, 152; wife, 151–52
Adam, 219, 263, 291
afterlife, 109–10, 114, 118, 129–30, 131
aging, 35–37, 89–90, 122, 123–24, 124, 125
AIDS, 111–13
alcoholism, 290
alienation, 52–53, 135, 137, 141, 147, 147–48, 155–56, 241, 243
All Saints Day, 49
anger, 21, 25–27, 75, 173, 227
assassination, 110–11, 154

Baldwin, James, 226
beauty, 35–37
birth, 67, 68–69, 198
Boaz, 265–66
body, 45, 49, 50, 207–8, 208–10, 212–13, 216, 217
bread, baking, 187–88
breast-feeding, 48

Cain and Abel, 263
cancer, 123
Chain of Being, 246
change, 23, 29, 32–33, 120–21, 121–22, 138–39, 144–45; social, 163–64, 166–67, 167–68, 170–71, 171–72, 175, 177
childhood, remembrance of, 54
children, 76, 99–100, 167
choir, church, 224–25
Christmas, 55, 140. See also Jesus, birth of
church, 190–91, 194, 199, 241
co-dependence, 25–27, 31–32, 34–35
comfort, 175
coming of age, 28, 71–72, 72–73, 79, 94, 95
commitment, 181
communication, 42–43, 138
communion, sacrament of, 42–43, 138

compassion, 122
cooking, 83, 202–3, 231, 285
courage, 123
crime, 144
crucifixion, 211, 256, 272–73, 273–74
cycles of life, 98–99

dancing, 233–34
daughter, 28, 71–72, 72–73, 73–74, 79, 93–94, 275–76, 286
death, 23, 49, 99–100, 123–24, 126, 127, 129–30, 232–33, 243, 249, 276; of brother, 118; of child, 114–15; of the elderly, 126; of father, 113–14; of grandmother, 91, 118–19; of husband, 114; of lover, 120; of maiden aunt, 115–16; of mother, 116, 117; of parent, 93
Delilah, 269
depression, 30–31
dishwashing, 201–2
divorce, 135–36
doctor, 30–31
Dubois, W.E.B., 241

Easter, 110–11, 212
ecology, 136–37, 178–79
Eden, 235, 263
empathy, 41–42
enemy, 227
environment. See ecology
eros, 45, 210–11
Eve, 263

faith, 96–97, 123–24, 256
family, 55–56
father, 92–93
fear, 23, 46, 129–30, 231–32
Feast of the Assumption of the Virgin, 273–74
First Communion, 188–89
foot-washing, 193–94
forgiveness, 29, 55, 114, 150–51, 224–25
friendship, 57–58, 144–45
Frog and the Prince, 276–77

gardening, 161–62, 171–72, 242
generations, 85–86, 88–89, 91–92,
  93–94, 230
God, 27, 57–58, 199, 200–201, 207, 211,
  213, 214, 215–16, 225–26, 239, 240,
  241, 245, 247–48, 249, 250–51,
  256–57, 259, 264–66, 268, 269,
  272–73; in nature, 252–53, 254, 255
Goddess, 228, 241, 242–43, 244, 245–47,
  249–50, 278, 287
grandfather, 108–9
grandmother, 30, 83–84, 86, 87–91, 230
grandparents, 85
grieving, 105–6, 113–14, 127, 128, 131,
  161–62

Hansel and Gretel, 277–78
healing, 30–31, 51–52
Heidegger, Martin, 93
help, asking for, 37
Hiroshima and Nagasaki, 177, 178–79,
  288–89
Holocaust, 163, 174
Holy Spirit, 56, 176, 183, 217, 240, 258,
  282
homeless, 52–53, 143–44
homemaking, 285
hope, 181–82, 183
housewife, 147–48
hug, 52–53
hunting, 230–31

idolatry, 27
image of women, false cultural, 21–22
Immaculate Conception, 198
immigrant, 87, 140, 142–43, 223
incarnation, 251
incest, 135
inclusive language, 278
independence, 27
infertility, 66–67, 122
intimacy, 45, 48, 49, 50, 51, 55–56
ironing, 55–56
isolation. See alienation

Jesus, 163–64, 193, 197, 198–99, 212,
  256, 272–73; birth of, 198, 271
Joan of Arc, 272, 274–75
Job's wife, 163, 267
John, Saint, 285
Joseph, 272
journey, 164
joy, 200–201, 210
justice, 173, 181

Kali, 249–50
King, Jr., Martin Luther, 110–11, 241

Last Judgment, 254
Lazarus, 271
Lilith, 30–31
listening, 42–43
loneliness, 32–33, 47, 52–53, 140, 263
Lord's Supper, 193
loss, 128–29, 130, 140
Lot's wife, 267
love, 27, 41, 43–44, 45, 48, 52–53,
  55–59, 130, 137, 146, 181, 196, 233,
  250; comfort of, 48, 49; family, 54,
  55–56
love-making, 45–46, 47, 50, 207–8, 214,
  215, 257
Luther, Martin, 281

Malcolm X, 241
male / female, 27, 41–42, 42–43, 44, 147,
  149, 149–50, 235, 248
marriage, 147–48, 149
Mary Magdalene, 193
Mary, mother of Jesus, 198, 240, 271, 272,
  273–74
masculinity, image of, 42
masks, 25
mastectomy, 123
menstruation, 94, 95, 213
mental illness, 97, 180
mermaid, 279
minister, 199
ministry, 248
miracle, 197
miscarriage, 106–7
mother, 30, 48, 69–70, 74–78, 91–92,
  93–94, 95–96, 230, 263, 275–76
motherhood, 169–70
mothering, 71, 74, 76, 194, 285
Muse, 292–93, 293–95

naming, 287–88
Nebuchadnezzar, 268
New Year, 29

Oedipus, 278
omnipotence, 257
ordination, of women, 217, 248

parenting, 76, 95–96, 98, 162–63, 291
Paris and Helen, 44
patience, 159
patriarchy, 241, 244
peace, 55, 59, 169–70
pornography, 226–27
poverty, 54, 143–44, 167–68, 223–24,
  290–91
praise, 207–8
prayer, 169, 176–77, 201–2, 216, 244,
  248, 255

predestination, 165
pregnancy, 63, 64–65, 65–66, 68–69

quilts, 128, 135, 164–65

racism, 153–54, 155, 226–27
rape, 85, 97, 150–51
Red Riding Hood, 275–76
relationship, 285; egalitarian, 235–36
relatives, 96–97
relinquishment, 123–24, 128–29
rest home, 124–25
resurrection, in nature, 115–16, 126, 253–54, 271
Romeo and Juliet, 278–79
Ruth and Naomi, 264–66

sacrament, 212, 216
salvation, 129, 192–93, 207, 211
Samson, 269
Sarah, 264, 265
sea, 121–22
Seboulisa, 243
self-acceptance, 22, 23–24, 25, 34–35
self-confidence, 23–24, 34–35, 159
self-identity, 21, 22, 25–27, 28–29, 240, 250–51
sensuality, Divine nature of, 207, 213, 216
Shadrach, Meshach, and Abednego, 268
Sheba, 269
silence, 255
sin, 246
Solstice, 138
son, 69–70, 77–78

spring, 212, 216
starvation, 167–68, 246
stillborn, 105–6
suicide, 97, 108–9, 109–10, 140, 252; attempted, 147–48, 230, 233
sunrise, 218–19

thanksgiving, 200–210, 227–29, 241
time, 50
transformation, 187–88
transition. See change
truth, 159–60, 187; speaking the, 42–43, 178–79, 180

urban living, 56–57, 143–44, 146, 160, 162–63, 223–24

values, false, 161, 166
violence, 96–97, 138, 141–42, 144, 150–55, 161
virgin birth, 198
vulnerability, 160; of God, 211, 257–58

war, 177, 178–79, 288–89
Watts, 155
wedding, 189–90, 214–15
words, sacredness of, 285, 287–88, 291, 297
work, 41, 142, 172–73, 243
writing, 76, 123, 177, 285, 287, 288–89, 290–91, 293–95

Yom Kippur, 155–56